# RUNECASTER'S HANDBOOK

# RUNECASTER'S HANDBOOK

## The Well of Wyrd

### Edred Thorsson

WEISERBOOKS
San Francisco, CA / Newburyport, MA

First published in 1999 by
Red Wheel/Weiser, LLC
With offices at
665 Third Street, Suite 400
San Francisco, CA 94107
www.redwheelweiser.com

ISBN: 978-1-57863-136-0

Library of Congress Cataloging-in-Publication Data

Thorsson, Edred
    [At the Well of Wyrd]
    Runecaster's handbook : the Well of Wyrd / Edred Thorsson
       p.     cm.
    Originally published: At the Well of Wyrd. York Beach, Me. : S. Weiser, 1988.
    Includes bibliographical references (p.   ) and index.
    ISBN 1-57863-136-X (paper : alk. paper)
    1. Fortune-telling by runes   I. Title.
  BF1891.R85T56  1999
  133.3'3--dc21                  99-22822
                                 CIP

Cover design by Claudine Mansour
Typeset in 11 point Goudy

Printed in the United States of America
MV
15 14 13 12 11 10 9 8 7

For Nancy

# Contents

# Acknowledgments

Thanks go to Robert Zoller, James Chisholm,
and Mitchell Edwin Wade for their help in
researching the art of runecasting.

# Preface

This volume is one of three in what has become a trilogy of runic handbooks. The other two, *Futhark: A Handbook of Rune Magic* and *Runelore: A Handbook of Esoteric Runology*, also are published by Samuel Weiser, Inc. In all of these books an effort has been made to combine the most traditional forms available with what we have been able to learn about the spiritual world of the ancient Germanic peoples through painstaking scholarly research galvanized by rational intuition.

Although the runic tradition is one full of innovative techniques, I have made a general practice in this book to stick to techniques, models of operation, and patterns of meaning for which we have good evidence within the old runic traditions. Innovation is encouraged, but at the level where it is most appropriate, with the individual. The sacred art of runic divination has been the most abused aspect of the tradition during this current runic revival. Perhaps this volume can begin to restore it. The approach to the Well of Wyrd can be the holy road to the depths of the self and it is to this end that the book is dedicated. Those interested in continuing runic research are invited to write to:

The Rune-Gild
P.O. Box 7622
Austin, TX 78713
USA

# Introduction

To communicate directly with a god, or the gods – that is what divination is all about. The runes on their most mundane level are a writing system. On both the mundane and the cosmic levels they are a system of communication. They are tools for reading otherwise hidden truths. Runes are a sort of traditional code, originally the gift of the god Ódhinn (Woden), through which messages can be sent from one level of reality to another, from one world to another. Whether in magic (*galdr*), where the runester's aim is to cause the objective world to conform to subjective will, or in runecasting, where the runester's aim is to read the hidden truths of his or her own subjective being or of the objective worlds, the runes are used as tools – as media – by which messages may be sent and received.

In reality, of course, the true runes dwell within the soul of the runester – within *you*. The runestaves are symbolic objects which act as a kind of magical mirror of your soul. When you gaze upon the runestaves strewn on the holy cloth of white, you are truly gazing deep within the Well of Wyrd. As a runecaster, the vitki approaches the level of a priest or priestess (of a *godhi* or *gydhja*), someone charged to deal with the gods and to act as a communicator between the worlds of the gods and that of Midhgardhr. Most important, however, is the fact that anyone who takes the time to become skilled in runecasting will open unseen channels between the conscious and unconscious selves.

This "opening of channels" is won only after some effort and willpower have been spent. The would-be runecaster must learn much and work much before great success can be expected. In this book, together with information to be found in *Futhark* and

*Runelore*, you will find all that you will ever need to become an effective "runic communicator."

This book is intended to be a practical manual containing concrete indications of exact traditional lore and procedures; but it is not overly restrictive. Where the elder tradition is clear, we follow it, but in some technical matters we have had to reconstruct some details. This was done in the spirit of the Germanic and runic tradition. Each detail can be supported by some aspect or interpretation of the older tradition as it has survived in historical or literary sources. However, it is also an integral part of the Germanic and runic tradition to innovate where necessary. The potentially great runecaster will not hesitate to invent new forms or rune readings, casting methods, etc. Most runecasters – and would-be experts on the subject – do not err on the side of innovation, but depend too much on unthinking, rote borrowing from some other (usually later, more "popular") system of divination. These borrowed elements then are shoved willy-nilly into the runic system.

Another problem often encountered in books on "runic divination" is that the writer is totally ignorant of the true tradition – and prefers to remain so. The quality of your runecasts will be greater if you invest the time and energy to learn something before you begin casting (much less writing!).

Runic divination needs to be practiced before you can become skilled. This will require that you make many castings which probably will be undertaken with only a modicum of passion. You are urged not to make runecasting a profane form of "play" (for entertainment purposes); to this end the rituals should help. However, from a practical standpoint, how can you expect yourself to become proficient if you only undertake runecasts on important occasions? In the beginning, daily practice should be observed, though it is probably wisest not to undertake more than one casting per day. In this balanced way, a healthy respect for the runes, along with initiated familiarity will be gained in the shortest possible time.

Sometimes the runecaster poses a question to the runes, but the runes seem to be speaking to another point. The runes (i.e., your personal *inner* runes) tend to pick up the real question on your mind or in your heart. It is easiest to get accurate readings from these kinds of questions. More refined questions require more direction of the conscious will.

All in all, runecasting itself is perhaps the best method of "getting to know" the runes. Reading—even memorizing—what the elder tradition says or what you find in *Futhark* and *Runelore* is fine, but the direct method of runester to runes is by far the most powerful way of learning about the "mysteries." Skills in runecasting can be applied directly to all other aspects of rune-work and runecraft.

The tide has turned and the time has come for all the kith and kin of Ódhinn to gather at the Well of Wyrd again to read the ordeal of the gods and humanity and to handle the mighty blood-tines.

# 1

# Historical Background

THE WORD "RUNE" SIMPLY MEANS "mystery" or "secret." The basic meaning is the same in all the ancient Germanic dialects: Old Norse *rún*, Old High German *rūna*, Old English *rūn*, and Gothic *rūna*. The word probably goes back to a root having something to do with vocal performance – a whisper or a roar. In any case, the association with a written character or graph is secondary. It refers first and foremost to an idea or principle, expressed orally and/or in a magical utterance, and secondly to a visual representation of that principle.

When the Germanic peoples began writing in the same manner as the Greeks and Romans, they called the graphs with which they performed this task "runes." Each rune represented a mystery, and a certain principle of esoteric lore was attached to it. (This is not surprising since the people who developed and maintained this system were also the custodians of other intellectual and religious material in the culture.) Beyond this, the system itself could be used to represent natural language and thus phonetically preserve the magical formulas themselves. These runes—or runestaves—became "whisperers of secrets." Through them—silently and over great spans of time and distance—communication could be effected. Symbolically, this could also be said of their ability to effect communication between the very realms of existence—from gods to humans, from humans to gods and even to the natural realms.

The importance of this should be obvious to anyone who is interested in either magic or divination. The runes, although not a language in the usual sense of the word, do constitute a metalanguage. A metalanguage is a symbolic system through which meaning can be transmitted above and beyond that of which the natural language is capable. Poetry also does this. Indeed, classic Germanic poetry very likely grew out of runic divinatory practices.

By means of this metalanguage the runecaster can carry out a meaningful dialogue with his or her environment—inner and outer. This aspect is at the root of the real meaning of the word "rune." Also, all this makes much more sense when understood within the ancient Germanic cosmology of multiple worlds—and their psychology of multiple souls.[1]

## Runic History

In the most exoteric historical sense, the runes represent an "alphabet" used in an unbroken tradition by the Germanic peoples from ancient times to as late as the early twentieth century in remote areas of Scandinavia. This continuous tradition went through many transformations, however. It is important to realize that the runes, although a system of symbols (a metalan-

---

[1] Edred Thorsson, *Runelore: A Handbook of Esoteric Runology* (York Beach, ME: Samuel Weiser, 1987): 167-173.

guage), do not constitute a language in the usual sense. Any natural language (e.g., English, Russian, Japanese) theoretically could be written in runestaves, though historically the runes were never employed outside the Germanic group of languages, i.e., they were never used by the Celts or Finns.

The oldest runic tradition is that of the twenty-four-stave or Elder Futhark. This system may have begun as early as 200 B.C.E., but certainly was in use by the first century C.E. (The oldest inscription found to date is the Meldorf brooch, which dates from about 50 C.E.) In Scandinavia this system continued in an unbroken stream until around 800 C.E. when it was systematically reformed into the sixteen-stave or Younger Futhark. Within the time frame of the Elder Futhark (beginning as early as 450 C.E.) an extended twenty-eight-stave futhorc was developed in Frisian and Anglo-Saxon territories. This system continued to be expanded and extensively represented in more diverse media (in manuscripts) until around 1050. Also within the formal tradition of the twenty-four-stave futhark there was a South Germanic runic tradition which flourished in the sixth and seventh centuries C.E., especially in Bavaria, Alemania, and Thuringia.

In Scandinavia the vigorous sixteen-stave futhark system, which had begun at the dawn of the so-called Viking Age, was slowly being corrupted by the southern European alphabetic system. The runestaves were taken out of their distinctive futhark order and put into an alphabetic one. This alphabetic reform was more or less complete for most exoteric purposes by about 1300. However, the rune poems show that the esoteric tradition of the futhark order survived into the fifteenth century.

Knowledge of the runestaves as a writing system all but died out everywhere except in Scandinavia, where it continued to be an alternative utilitarian script (especially for carvings) among clerics, merchants, and farmers. Eventually runelore was only preserved in the most remote interior areas of Scandinavia.

For a more detailed history, of runic developments the reader should consult *Runelore*.[2]

## Runecasting in History and Literature

Without the written sources, especially Old Norse and Latin texts, it would be difficult to determine the nature of historical runecasting in any scientific way. These accounts, and certain words used in them, give us many clues to the structure of runic divinatory ritual and provide contexts for acts of divination in general. There are, however, limits to this evidence. First, these texts only became common in the Middle Ages, and although they surely represent much older material and reflect archaic practices, we should be aware of this time discrepancy. Second, the saga accounts are integrated into narrative tales and may have some degree of literary convention built into them. Both of these points, however, are minor when viewed in the broad scope of the tradition.

There are no clear examples in the archaeological record of runestaves carved for divinatory purposes, but most likely this is due to the fact that they were scratched on perishable materials. Or, perhaps, they were ritually destroyed after use as a matter of normal procedure. It is another surprising fact that there are no direct, non-mythological references to the act of runecasting in Old Norse literature. Despite all this, and chiefly based on linguistic evidence and parallel accounts in historical texts, we can be fairly certain that the practice was known.

Linguistic evidence is of two kinds: (1) words for the tools or runecasting, and (2) terms which originally must have been characterizations of the results of runecastings.

Actual pieces of wood upon which individual runes or runic combinations were carved (and usually colored with blood or

---

[2]Edred Thorsson, *Runelore: A Handbook of Esoteric Runology* (York Beach, ME: Samuel Weiser, 1987): 3–51.

red dye) were known in Old Norse as *hlaut-teinar* (sg. *hlaut-teinn*) or lot-twig (also interpreted by Snorri Struluson as "blood-twigs"), and *hlaut-vidhar*, lot-woods. The original use of the Germanic term *stabaz*, meaning stave or stick, perhaps had to do with the fact that runes were carved on pieces of wood that most probably were used in divinatory practices. The Germanic terms *runō* and *stabaz* were so intertwined by this practice that the words eventually became synonymous. An interesting piece of corroborating evidence is found in the Old English word *wyrd-stæf*, stave of wyrd or weird, which seems to be an obvious reference to divinatory usage.

Old Germanic dialects are full of compound words which refer to various types of runes/staves. Some are technical descriptions (ON *málrúnar*, speech-runes; ON *blódhgar rúnar*, bloody runes; OHG *leod-rūna*, song-rune; etc.), while others give indications of the reasons for which they are to be worked (ON *brim-rúnar*, sea runes [to calm it]; *bjarg-rúnar*, birth runes [to help facilitate it]; etc.). However, among these there are some designations that appear to classify the results of a runecasting. Some are auspicious (ON *líkn-stafir*, health staves; ON *gaman-rúnar*, joy runes; ON *audh-stafir*, staves of riches; ON *sig-rúnar*, victory runes) while others seem inauspicious (ON *myrkir stafir*, dark staves; ON *böl-stafir*, evil staves; OE *beadu-run*, conflict rune; ON *flærdh-stafir*, deception staves). Of course, in many cases, the passive readings of these terms could be turned around to active workings.

As far as the actual practice of runecasting is concerned, the best description is provided by Tacitus writing in chapter 10 of the *Germania* (about 98 C.E.). Formerly, there might have been a debate as to whether the *notae*, signs, mentioned by him actually could have been runes, since the oldest inscription was thought to date from about 150 C.E. The discovery of the Meldorf brooch (about 50 C.E.), however, provided hard evidence that the runes were known from before the time when the *Germania* was written. The account by Tacitus may be translated:

To the taking of auspices and drawing of lots they pay as much attention as any one: the way they draw lots is uniform. A branch is cut from a nut-bearing tree and cut into slips: these are designated by certain signs (Latin *notae*) and thrown randomly over a white cloth. Afterwards, the priest of state, if the consultation is a public one, or the father of the family, if it is private, offers a prayer to the gods, and while looking up into the sky, takes up three slips, one at a time, and interprets their meaning from the signs carved on them. If the message forbids something, no further inquiry is made on the question that day; but if it allows something, then further confirmation is required through the taking of auspices.[3]

In *The Conquest of Gaul* (Book I, 53) Caesar, writing in about 58 B.C.E., also mentions "consulting the lots three times" (*ter sortibus consultum*), so this must have been an important aspect of Germanic divination.[4]

Three Eddic passages also give significant magical – and rather cryptic – insight into runic divinatory practices. All occur in mythic contexts. In the "Völuspá," st. 20: "(the norns) scored on wood, they laid laws, they chose lives, they spoke the 'fates'" (ON *ørlög*). While in the "Hávamál," st. 80, we are told that "it is proven when you ask of the runes, which are sprung from the gods" (ON *regin*, divine advisors). In the "Hávamál," st. 111, there is the instructive passage:

> It is the time to sing
> on the stool of the theal
> at the well of Wyrd –
> I saw and I thought
> I saw and I spoke

[3]Translated from Rudolf Much, *Die Germania des Tacitus*, 2nd ed. (Heidelberg: Carl Winter, 1967): 129. See also Cornelius Tacitus, *The Argicola and the Germania* (Harmondsworth, UK: Penguin, 1948): 109-110.

[4]Julius Caesar, *The Conquest of Gaul* (Harmondsworth, UK: Penguin, 1951): 73.

*heeded the lore of Hár*
*of runes I heard it spoke*
*nor thought I of readings*
*at the hall of Hár*
*in the hall of Hár*
*so I heard it said.*

This passage not only gives indication of the objective picture of what the ritual procedures were–as Tacitus the outsider also could do–but it also gives us insight into the subjective, inner processes within the mind of the runecaster. This is something only an insider, only someone who was actually skilled in rune-casting, could have done.

There are other historical accounts by Christian observers which tell us little more than that the number three was of great importance.

## Runic Divination and the Magical Revival

In this century, many systems of runic divination have appeared in the world. Only one of them, that presented in *Rune Games*, by Marijane Osborn and Stella Longland,[5] has even come close to being a traditional system. However, in Germany, systems inspired by the trail-blazing work of Guido von List (1848-1919) have become a virtual neo-tradition within various schools of magic.

Most of the major writers on rune magic in the early Listian tradition did not explicitly address matters of runic divination. The one exception was E. Tristan Kurtzahn, whose *Die Runen als Heilszeichen und Schicksalslose* [The Runes as Holy Signs and Lots of Fate] (1924)[6] included an appendix on specific methods

---

[5]Marijane Osborn and Stella Longland, *Rune Games* (London: Routledge and Kegan Paul, 1982).
[6]E. Tristan Kurtzahn, *Die Runen als Heilszeichen und Schicksalslose* (Bad Oldesloe: Uranus, 1924).

of runic divination—which he indicates he was reluctant to include. After the Second World War, Karl Spiesberger's book *Runenmagie* (1955)[7] included a whole chapter on "Runen-Mantik" (to a large extent drawn from Kurtzahn's work). A sidelight to runic divination proper also was presented in 1955 by Roland Dionys Jossé in his *Die Tala der Raunen (Runo-astrologische Kabbalistik)*,[8] the subtitle of which translates: "a handbook of the interpretation of the essence and path of a person on the basis of the runes of fate concealed in his name." This is a type of runo-numerology based on a modification of the Listian system. The most recent foray into runic divination in this tradition is the comprehensive treatment by Werner Kosbab in *Das Runen-Orakel* (1982).[9]

In the English-speaking worlds we have not fared so well. As early as the late 1950s runic divination seems to have been known in occult circles, but since that time, and for the most part, only what can be described as bastardizations of the runic traditions have found their way into print in English. Unfortunately, and perhaps typically, one of the "offenders" in this regard is also the one most widely distributed: Ralph Blum's *The Book of Runes*.[10] Several other "systems" have been generated within the Anglo-American occult mill (see bibliography), but I believe only one, *Rune Games*, is worth considering by readers interested in tradition or authenticity. Osborn and Longland present a picture of a system and a culture in transition—from the heathen to the Christian. This may be seen as a reversed image of the present situation as the cultural pendulum swings back. *At the Well of Wyrd* tries to present a totally traditional,

---

[7]Karl Spiesberger, *Runenmagie* (Berlin: Schikowski, 1955).

[8]Roland Dionys Jossé, *Die Tala der Raunen* (Freiburg/Breisgau: Bauer, 1955).

[9]Werner Kosbab, *Das Runen-Orakel* (Freiburg/Breisgau: Bauer, 1982).

[10]Ralph Blum, *The Book of Runes* (New York: St. Martin's Press, 1982). Blum's rune game has opened up the realm of runes for many novices; however, those who go on to become serious students of runology find that the rune game disregards the essentials of the whole futhark system. So despite whatever valuable personal insights Blum is able to provide on individual runes, his whole system must unfortunately be regarded as artificial.

pre- (and post!) Christian system for those who are ready to throw away their crutches.

Although the present text contains a complete system of viable runic divination that can be used by persons of differing traditions, it remains a significant part of the work of the Rune-Gild to teach deeper, even more traditional methods of rune-casting, and to continue research in this field. Divination is an important tool not only in runework (esoteric self-transformation) but also in runecraft (esoteric environmental engineering).

# 2

# Runic Divinatory Theory

THE UNDERSTANDING OF HOW RUNECASTING works can be a relative thing. How we understand it may be different from the exact ways in which an Erulian runecaster of ancient times might have explained it. There are also various levels of understanding in our own times. So why even bring up "theory"? Why not just "practice" and not worry about such matters?

From the standpoint of true runework on any level these questions are, of course, absurd. It is in the character of the runester to inquire and act, to seek further into the runes. If the runes are to be more than a "fortune-telling" system—which they must be—then working through various levels of understanding of them can only be enhanced by constant attempts to understand them in ever more comprehensive ways. So, the question of "theory," or understanding, is actually a practical one.

Traditionally, runecasting is a true act of direct communication between humans and the divinities of the many realms, as described in *Runelore* (chapter 6).[1] This communication takes place in the metalanguage of the gods (runes) – the outer form of the Gift of Ódhinn. The runestaves and all the lore attendant to them as well as the ritual methods of consulting them also were known to be of divine origin. The first "runecaster" was Ódhinn himself, and in casting the runes the diviner is actually partici- pating in the divine process in an imitative way. This is the essence of the traditional theory of runecasting, at least from an Odian point of view. The non-Odian populace of ancient times would have seen the divinatory process as one in which "the gods speak to mortals," and in this they probably were encour- aged by the Odians.

This exoteric understanding – as all true levels of understanding – is not at all incorrect. However, what this level fails to see is that in the context of the ritual act the runecaster has assumed the status of "a god." Actually, in order to commu- nicate with the hidden transpersonal reality (the runes) the runester must assume this status in order to be totally effective. The results of the casting then are communicated to the rune- caster's own human level of consciousness (and perhaps to that of others) through the runestaves and their lore. Therefore, runecasting is not a totally passive undertaking. The runester's will, ability, knowledge, and level of being are very important. Without them the runes would remain forever hidden.

Another aspect of traditional theory involves the "divinities of fate," which are numerous and prevalent in Germanic lore. These can be roughly divided into three "functions" or charac- teristic realms of activity. First, the Great Norns (ON *Nornir*) Urdhr, Verdhandi, and Skuld give the overall context in which action and reaction, cause and effect, time, and synchronicity exist, and provide the context in which they can be compre- hended. Second are the personal "bearers of fate." These are conceptualized as the entities who are attached to an individual

---

[1]Edred Thorsson, *Runelore: A Handbook of Esoteric Runology* (York Beach, ME: Samuel Weiser, 1987): 71–85.

and who carry that individual's fate (ON *ørlög*), thus influencing his or her life and actions. To some extent the runecaster is seeking knowledge of these entities and their contents. Entities that belong to this second group include the fetch (ON *fylgja*) and *nornir* (lesser norns), as well as in certain instances *valkýrjur* (valkyries) and *disir* (dises).[2] Third are the "guides." These entities are thought to manipulate the runelots to fall or to be laid out in certain ways. Guides may be norns, dises, or even valkyries. It might be noted that from the Odian standpoint these entities are actually parts of the whole self of the Odian.


THE RUNES AND FATE

The *perthro*-rune is fundamental to the understanding of the context in which runic divination works. This rune contains the secret workings of the three Great Norns – Urdhr-Verdhandi-Skuld. These are vast forces of the cosmos whose manifestation is synonymous with the origin of time (including synchronicity), motion (thus cause and effect), and all becoming. These are dark etin-forces according to "Völuspá," st. 8, in the *Poetic Edda*.

The essence of their mystery is contained in the meanings of their names. Urdhr (OE *Wyrd*) is simply the past participle of the verb *verdha*, to become; turn (OE *wyrd* is similarly formed from the verb *weordhan*). So Urdhr really means "that which has become or turned," – in other words, "the past." Verdhandi is the present participle of the same verb, and so means "that which is becoming or turning," i.e., "the present." Skuld obviously comes from another verb, *skulu*, meaning shall. It is essentially, or qualitatively, different from the other two, and means "that which shall (be)." In Old Norse this has connotations of duty and obligation, but in the most archaic levels when the term first arose it merely indicated that which should come to pass, given past circumstances.

---

[2]Edred Thorsson, *Runelore: A Handbook of Esoteric Runology* (York Beach, ME: Samuel Weiser, 1987): 170.

It is also of the greatest importance to realize that the old Germanic idea of time was built on a past vs. non-past model. If you will notice, even our modern English does not really have a future tense (it needs the auxiliary verb *will* to form this tense). This is a feature common to the Germanic languages—German, English, Dutch, and the Scandinavian dialects. But we do have a real past tense. This is because to the Germanic mind the past is real, the future is only hypothetical and subject· to change, and the present is an ever-becoming now.

If those concepts are fully understood, it will be easy to see the true nature of the Germanic concept of "fate" (ON *ørlög*). *Ørlög* is not a set and immutable thing—in fact, it is being transformed constantly by ongoing action. However, *ørlög* is a powerful force and one from whose grasp few can escape once certain patterns of action become ingrained. The well-known Germanic "fatalism" is, for the most part, an exoteric understanding of this process. Your "Skuld" is affected—even determined—by "Urdhr," your Wyrd. Wyrd is essentially "past action" which has been formulated and absorbed by your being. Now, if to this already vast web-work the idea of Germanic "reincarnation" (ON *aptrburdhr*, rebirth) is added, a truly complex image arises. Wyrd seems (indeed is) so compelling because its roots are usually hidden in their remote "pastness"; they are so deeply ingrained in us that they have become invisible. Also, the sheer complexity of the web-work of wyrd, all of the past actions and reactions on all levels of being throughout the entire time of your "essential existences," make sorting out the threads of wyrd enormously difficult. On the most elementary level the power of wyrd can be expressed in the phrase "Old habits are hard to break." Through runecasting, the vitki endeavors to get at the root or Wyrd-level of the matter under question.

Two technical terms mentioned above probably need further analysis. *Aptrburdhr* or rebirth (ON) is a process whereby the essential powers and characteristics of a person are handed down to, and inherited by, later generations. This usually happens naturally and along genetic lines; e.g., the grandson is the reincarnation of the dead grandfather. With this rebirth the grandson also "inherits" the fate (ørlög) of the grandfather and of his whole clan or tribe. The child is affected by its heritage.

Ørlög itself is a complex idea. The word literally means "primal layers" or "primal laws," and really indicates action that has been "laid down" in the past. But ørlög cuts two ways. It is both the past actions that we have dealt out (in this and perhaps in the previous existences of our essential selves), and that which others (or impersonal forces) have dealt out to us over the same span of time. In English the only survival of this concept is in the word *ordeal* (primal-deal), i.e., that which was "dealt out" in the past. Thus trials by ordeal (in theory) merely objectively demonstrated the truth based on these concepts.

From what has been said above, it should be clear that the process the runester sets out to investigate through runecastings is not strictly one of cause and effect. The nornic process is one that formulates a set of probabilities based on a whole range of complex actions and reactions on many levels of being. The runecasting is an attempt to reproduce an image of this webwork of wyrd so that its contents can be analyzed and read. The theory that comes closest to fitting the Germanic model is that of synchronicity, originated by the Swiss psychologist C. G. Jung.[3]

A *synchronicity* is a meaningful coincidence, when outer events (happenings) coincide with a psychic event (an awareness of meaning). These are moments in which the eternal fields of meaningfulness open up and touch upon moments in cyclical (natural) time. These are moments when our souls and all the world around us can be re-shaped to some extent – if we are aware of them.

Acts of runecasting are not so much attempts to predict future events as they are attempts to arrange inner and outer

---

[3]Carl G. Jung, *Synchronicity* (Princeton: Princeton University Press, 1973). See also Marie-Louise von Franz, *On Divination and Synchronicity* (Toronto: Inner City Books, 1980).

circumstances (the soul and the lay of the runestaves) in such a way that the center of the web-work of wyrd is made legible. From this center we are able to interpret the shape of much of the rest of the warp and weave of the world around us. We may even be able to see the whole world: past and "present," archetypal and mundane. Those who can read the runes will be able to expand their vision in such a way that all the conditioning factors of any situation are clarified. Lines in the web-work of wyrd can be extended in consciousness – and thus the realm of probabilities surrounding events yet to happen can come into view.

If the vitki considers the Yggdrasill pattern shown in *Runelore*[4] as a four-dimensional web-work, and the act of runecasting as a way of expanding consciousness out along all the wide ways into the nine worlds, then runecasting can be seen as a method of expanding awareness from a centerpoint (Midhgardhr). But just as Midhgardhr is the final fruit of the coming into being of the worlds of Yggdrasill, so too is it the seed from which new growth springs. Runecasting can give us the probable patterns for this new growth.

Finally, something needs to be said about the "experience of the wyrd." In our colloquial language the term "weird" has come to be synonymous with strange. The is an unfortunate turn of events. In former times, a "weird" experience was one which seemed to have its origins in the numinous, in the world of the gods. A weird experience caused the hair to rise on the back of the neck, and it was felt to be highly significant. Such events and feelings were more synchronistic than anything else. Things became palpably clear, sometimes causing a fearful reaction. It is hoped that this book will help in some way to rescue this word from the oblivion of meaningless modern usage.

---

[4]Edred Thorsson, *Runelore: A Handbook of Esoteric Runology* (York Beach, ME: Samuel Weiser, 1987): 154.

# 3

# Runic Symbolism and Divinatory Tables

IN *FUTHARK* AND IN *RUNELORE*, we concentrated on magical aspects or on general matters of lore; here we must concentrate on the keys to divinatory meaning. It must be emphasized, however, that the keys presented here do not exhaust the possibilities of runic readings. Each vitki ought to keep careful records of every casting so that personal trends in interpretation may be noted and utilized. Just as no two people really speak the same language (each of us uses grammar and vocabulary uniquely), the way in which "you and your runes communicate" also will be unique. This is why learning the runes is actually tantamount to learning to know the self.

The following tables, however, are based on traditional associations essentially drawn from insights into the rune poems and other aspects of ancient runelore (associations of names, number, etc.). Also, some advantage has been taken of the divinatory vision of the German Armanic system in which a great deal of runecasting has been practiced successfully for decades.

These tables will delineate the runic readings on three levels: (1) general lore, (2) "positive" or birth/life levels (under the heading "Bright-stave"), and (3) "negative" or death level (under the heading "Murk-stave"). The first is necessary to give a general orientation to the runic symbolism and to provide a context from which the runester will be able to expand personal readings. (It is in this regard that the information in *Futhark* and *Runelore* would be of greatest use.)

The "bright" reading of a rune is really its "normal" reading, the one it has in isolation and outside the context of other runes. This is by no means always "positive" in the sense of "beneficial." Take, for example, the runes *thurisaz, isa, nauthiz,* or *hagalaz,* all of which can be detrimental on their own in their "positive" aspects. The "negative" or murky reading of a rune is determined by its relationship to other runes or by the position in which it lands in a casting. This negativity is actually an expression of one of two possible patterns: (1) cataclysm, or (2) obstruction. When a rune is cataclysmically juxtaposed to another it indicates that change is in the offing, change that will perhaps be uncomfortable, but change that may lead to a new beginning. Obstruction of one runic force by another is the worst of possibilities; it suggests stasis and stagnation of the forces. Ways of determining the relative brightness or murkiness of a stave in any given reading will be discussed in detail in chapter 6.

Each table shows the stave shape, its numerical and phonetic values, its Germanic name with translations from various cultural and historical contexts, and the modern English word ultimately derived from it (or a reconstructed name). This English word can be used as an alternate modern name for the stave. Stanzas of the "Old English Rune Poem" (OERP), the "Old Norwegian Rune Rhyme" (ONRR), and the "Old Icelandic Rune Poem" (OIRP) that are relevant to each of the elder staves also are reproduced. There are only sixteen runes in the younger system used by the "Old Norwegian Rune Rhyme" and the "Old Icelandic Rune Poem," so only those sixteen of the twenty-four runes of the elder system have stanzas from these two works. The Latin gloss appended to each stanza of the OIRP is also provided along with a translation.

# 1.

Phonetic value: F

Germanic name: *Fehu*, mobile wealth, cattle, livestock, money, gold

Modern English: Fee

## OERP

*(Money) is a comfort
to everybody
although every man ought
to deal it out freely
if he wants to get approval
from the lord.*

## ONRR

*(Money) causes strife among kinsmen;
the wolf grows up in the woods.*

## OIRP

*(Money) is the (cause of) strife among kinsmen,
and the fire of the flood-tide
and the path of the serpent.*

*aurum:* gold

## LORE

This is the principle of mobile power—within nature, within the self, and within society. *Fehu* is a power that flows outward like fire from its course and must be circulated in order to be beneficial. This circulation of fire must be handled by the athlings with wisdom and foresight so they do not destroy themselves or others. The F-rune is a sign of the first vital fire of life and movement which ensures continuing change in the world.

## BRIGHT-STAVE

Foresight is needed. Wealth may be in the offing, but it must be used with wisdom and shared generously to avoid conflict. If used properly, social success will be won. This is also true of the "inner wealth" of knowledge. Share and your power will grow. The origin of this power of well-being is outside your present consciousness; the power is just welling up from below the surface. Ethical behavior based on wisdom and tradition is called for. There may be travel in the offing. Great energy is indicated as well as new beginnings and new life. Erotic renewal. This rune could signify a person who works with animals or finances.

## MURK-STAVE

Greed can cause you to become an outcast in society, and to suffer inner alienation from the self. Discord may be in the offing, discord based on a lack of circulation of the power of *fehu*. Excess of *fehu* can cause you to "burnout" your creative energies. Control them and use them with wisdom. There may be a proclivity toward offensive aggression. Obstruction leads to a blockage or atrophy of vital energies. Failure and poverty are in the offing.

## KEYWORDS FOR *FEHU*

**Bright**: Social success, Wealth energy, Foresight, New beginning

**Murky**: Greed, "Burnout," Atrophy, Poverty, Discord

# 2.

Phonetic value: U

Germanic name: *Uruz*, aurochs; drizzle, slag

Modern English: Urox

### OERP

*(Aurochs) is fearless
and greatly horned
a very fierce beast,
it fights with its horns,
a famous roamer of the moor
it is a courageous animal.*

### ONRR

*(Slag) is from bad iron;
oft runs the reindeer on the hard snow.*

### OIRP

*(Drizzle) is the weeping of clouds,
and the diminisher of the rim of ice,
and (an object for) the herdsman's hate.*

*umbre:* shadow (should read *imber*, shower)

### LORE

This is the principle of vital organic life energy, original procreation, and organic transformation. *Uruz* is the primal cosmic bovine-force that shapes manifestation and defends that manifested form. The aurochs was a wild and powerful large bison-like longhorned bovine that roamed Europe until it became extinct. The beast was known for its power, ferocity, and tenacity. The medieval rune poems use different meanings: (1) a purifying fire that removes dross elements, or (2) water that is forced from the clouds in a similar process.

## BRIGHT-STAVE

Vital strength is its essence. There is an emotive up-welling and out-pouring of energy. This energy leads to strength if it is tenaciously held onto and controlled. Properly this strength should be used to defend your "homeland," be that the physical home or the "hall" of the self (i.e., "defense mechanisms"). Strive toward inner goals and more power will result. Use the strength to burn away weakness and dross. Be constant and vigilant. The organic essence of the rune will lead to knowledge and understanding, health and general luck. (The horseshoe as a symbol of luck was derived from the : ᚢ : stave.) This rune could signify a physician or someone in the crafts.

## MURK-STAVE

Obsessive protectiveness and possessiveness. Misdirection of energy ruins or destroys other beneficial aspects. This can indicate strength used in the wrong way or time ("rain on the hay"), or strength used by the wrong people whose only desire is to control others ("shepherd"). Uncontrolled enthusiasm leads to mania. A blockage of *uruz* leads to sickness, inconsistency, and ignorance.

## KEYWORDS FOR *URUZ*

**Bright**: Strength, Defense, Tenacity, Freedom, Form, Health, Understanding

**Murky**: Weakness, Obsession, Misdirected force, Domination by others, Sickness, Inconsistency, Ignorance ·

# 3.

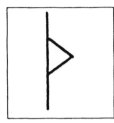

Phonetic value: TH

Germanic name: *Thurisaz*, giant (thurs); thorn

Modern English: Thurs or thorn

## OERP

*(Thorn) is very sharp;*
*for every thane*
*who grasps it; it is harmful,*
*and exceedingly cruel*
*to every man*
*who lies upon them.*

## ONRR

*(Thurs) causes the sickness of women;*
*few are cheerful from misfortune.*

## OIRP

*(Thurs) is the torment of women,*
*and the dweller in the rocks,*
*and the husband of Vardh-rúna (a giantess?)*

*Saturnus:* Saturn

## LORE

The thurs is a reactive force in brute nature. It is a reaction to the clash of two polarized forces and the transformation of that force into kinetic energy. This occurs in nature in the form of the thurses (unconscious forces), but also the Ása-Thórr makes use of an analogous force—Mjöllnir—to combat the encroachment of unconsciousness. The TH-rune is a sign of the psycho-sexual symbolic response, which in unconscious beings leads to compulsion but in conscious ones to transformation.

## BRIGHT-STAVE

Reactions to your deeds may be dangerous. Take care in passively engaging or blindly grasping the "outside world" (i.e., outside your self, home, etc.). Do so with knowledge. Danger may be present in the outside world. This is an erotic vital force. An intensification of erotic expression may be in the offing, but this may be mixed with pain. Correctly applied this power can be protective and lead to evolutionary change and regeneration. This is the rune of crisis for good or ill, a catalyst for change. It may represent an unskilled brutal person.

## MURK-STAVE

Unwisely approached, the TH-stave betokens defenselessness and danger. Beware of enemies from the outside. It indicates reactive complusion and misery in relations with the opposite sex. Betrayal may be in the offing. The thurs is an intellectually "dense" rock-like entity.

## KEYWORDS FOR THURS

**Bright**: Reactive force, Directed force, Vital eroticism, Regenerative catalyst

**Murky**: Danger, Defenselessness, Compulsion, Betrayal, Dullness

# 4.

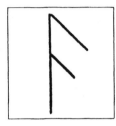

Phonetic value: A

Germanic name: *Ansuz*, the Ase, Ódhinn: sovereign ancestral god of the intellect

Modern English: Ans

## OERP

*(God/Mouth) is the chieftain*
*of all speech,*
*the mainstay of wisdom*
*and a comfort to the wise ones,*
*for every noble warrior*
*hope and happiness.*

## ONRR

*(Estuary) is the way of most journeys;*
*but the sheath is (that for) swords.*

## OIRP

*(Ase = Ódhinn) is the olden-father,*
*and Ásgardhr's chieftain,*
*and the leader of Valhöll.*

*Jupiter*: Jupiter

## LORE

This is the principle of divine conscious power as embodied in the god Ódhinn. Ódhinn is the divine pattern or exemplary model for self-transformation, not a god with whom worshippers seek "union." This is symbolically shown in the analogies made in the ONRR: estuary/ship-journey, and sword/scabbard. *Ansuz* contains the mystery of the "meta-language" as it embodies all linguistic and symbolic systems. This is the rune of synthetic consciousness.

## BRIGHT-STAVE

Skills involving language are indicated. The power of persuasion is great in the spoken word and the ability to imitate. Direct access to the source of consciousness and perhaps a transformative spiritual experience are in the offing. Learn the way of Ódhinn, but do not worship him. Responsibility to ancestral ways and the promotion of the interests of the ancestors are indicated. It is necessary to synthesize, to bring together disparate elements in order to understand. Inspiration and intellectual achievement are present. The unexpected must be expected. Strive for the best and highest. This rune may indicate an intellectual or priestly person.

## MURK-STAVE

Without proper understanding the *ansuz* may lead to delusion. Uncomfortable situations may be in the offing, as tests or catalysts to new understanding. Beware of attempts by others to manipulate you. Danger may come through a misuse of knowledge or from unwholesome influences. A blockage of this force leads to boredom and eventually to intellectual death.

## KEYWORDS FOR *ANSUZ*

**Bright:** Inspiration (enthusiasm), Synthesis, Transformation, Words

**Murky:** Misunderstanding, Delusion, Manipulation by others, Boredom

# 5.

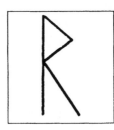

Phonetic value: R

Germanic name: *Raidho*, riding, vehicle

Modern English: Riding or Rowel

OERP

*(Riding) is in the hall*
*to every warrior*
*easy, but very hard*
*for the one who sits up*
*on a powerful horse*
*over miles of road.*

ONRR

*(Riding), it is said, is the worst for horses;*
*Reginn forged the best sword.*

OIRP

*(Riding) is a blessed sitting,*
*and a swift journey,*
*and the toil of the horse.*

*iter*: journey

LORE

This is the principle of rhythmic and proportional dynamism or energetic action. It is the cycle—but in spiral form—always governed by perfect proportion and interval. As such, *raidho* is the rune of the long ride, the long hard journey of growth and becoming in the world. This is a journey which must be governed by good rede (counsel) and a rational process. *Raidho* is the practice of what *ansuz* has inspired.

## BRIGHT-STAVE

An ordered change is indicated. Ordered ethical deeds are necessary. This requires planning, preparation, and good judgment, however. Action is necessary. Gain experience in the "outside world." The *fylgja* and *hamingja* must be strengthened. A journey or change in domestic situation is in the offing. Logical matters may become a concern. Justice may be expected. Make use of reason and good counsel. This rune may signify a person in the legal or transportation field.

## MURK-STAVE

Hard times are ahead. Spiritual crisis based on unpreparedness may be in the offing. Spiritual boredom resulting from rigid routines could ensue. Beware of bad advice. A blockage of the *raidho* force will lead to injustice, violence, stultification, or inappropriate irrationality.

## KEYWORDS FOR *RAIDHO*

**Bright:** Rationality, Action, Justice, Ordered growth, Journey

**Murky:** Crisis, Rigidity, Statsis, Injustice, Irrationality

# 6.

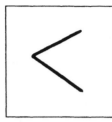

Phonetic value: K

Germanic name: *Kenaz*, torch; or *kaunaz*, sore

Modern English: Keen

## OERP

*(Torch) is to every living person
known by its fire,
it is clear and bright
it usually burns
when the athlings
rest inside the hall.*

## ONRR

*(Sore) is the curse of children;
grief makes a man pale.*

## OIRP

*(Sore) is the bale of children,
and a scourge,
and the house of rotten flesh.*

*flagella:* whip

## LORE

This is the principle of analysis (of breaking up things into their component parts) and of creativity, or shaping things. *Kenaz* is the fire of divine inspiration under the control of human craft, which results in artistic creation. It is the fire of the torch, the hearth, the harrow (altar), the forge, and the funeral pyre.

BRIGHT-STAVE

Inner creativity and artistry, or general ability and aptitude are indicated. Rest and relaxation are necessary to allow it to arise. The creative fire is applied to the personality. Transformation is suggested, a shaping or reshaping of the present situation, enlightened by divine inspiration. A child may be in the offing. This rune may indicate a person in the arts or crafts.

MURK-STAVE

Unwanted dissolution, perhaps in the form of physical disease or the break-up of a relationship. Problems with children may be indicated. Blockage of the *kenaz* force leads to inability and a lack of creativity or skill.

KEYWORDS FOR *KENAZ*

**Bright**: Technical ability, Inspiration, Creativity, Transformation, Offspring

**Murky**: Disease, Break-up, Inability, Lack of creativity

# 7.

Phonetic value: G

Germanic name: *Gebo*, gift, generosity

Modern English: Gift

## OERP

 (Gift) is for every man
a pride and praise,
help and worthiness;
and of every homeless adventurer
it is the estate and substance
for those who have nothing else.

## LORE

This is the principle of the three-fold Gift of Ódhinn: conscious-ness, divine breath, and form. It is also the principle of giving and taking, of an exchange between any two beings or two realms. It is the sacrifice—or gift—made by people to gods in order to compensate or petition for divine favors. In human society this is reflected as simple hospitality.

## BRIGHT-STAVE

Provide for hospitality and generosity with guests. Be prepared to accept it as well. A material or spiritual gift may be in the offing. You may expect great credit, honor, dignity—or you might be called upon to bestow these on another if you are in a position of power. You may have a magical exchange with a member of the opposite sex. A powerful and synchronistic

(Wyrd) experience could be in the offing. This rune may represent a person who works for a non-profit organization or charity, or someone in the hotel or restaurant business.

## MURK-STAVE

Take care not to give away all you have. Spend wisely. Do not become overly dependent upon gifts from others, for "aye does a gift always look for gain." An attempt to buy influence with gifts is possible; beware of financial enslavement. Things might get worse before they get better. Blockage of the *gebo* will cause greed and weakness, or poverty and loneliness.

## KEYWORDS FOR *GEBO*

**Bright**: Gift (giving), Generosity, Magical exchange, Honor, Sacrifice

**Murky**: Influence-buying, Greed, Loneliness, Dependence, Over-sacrifice

# 8.

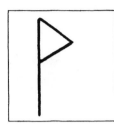

Phonetic value: W

Germanic name: *Wunjo*, joy

Modern English: Wyn

## OERP

*(Joy) is had*
*by the one who knows few troubles*
*pains and sorrows,*
*and to him who himself has*
*power and blessedness,*
*and a good enough house.*

## LORE

This is the principle of ideal harmonization of entities or elements—especially those derived from the same source. From this, harmony, joy, and good cheer naturally arise.

## BRIGHT-STAVE

Social and domestic harmony can be expected. Separation from pain or the ability to cope with it is indicated. Keep ideals in mind; strive for them. Either good physical health is indicated, or attention should be paid to it. Strive to bring together disparate elements in your life; organize things. Harmonize your inner and outer lives. New social relationships—not necessarily sexual ones—are likely. Material prosperity may result from business relationships. A person in social services may be signified by this rune.

## MURK-STAVE

Stultification of the individuality in the "group mind" is suggested. Blurring of individual efforts and minimalization of the individual ego can lead to loss of identity. Stoppage of the *wunjo* force results in poor relationships with others—strife and alienation—as well as inner alienation from the self and from the gods.

## KEYWORDS FOR *WUNJO*

**Bright**: Harmony, Joy, Fellowship, Prosperity

**Murky**: Stultification, Sorrow, Strife, Alienation

## 9.

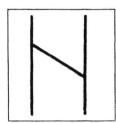

Phonetic value: H

Germanic names: *Hagalaz*, hail(-stone)

Modern English: Hail

**OERP**

(Hail) is the whitest of grains,
it comes from high in heaven
showers of wind hurl it,
then it turns to water.

**ONRR**

(Hail) is the coldest of grains;
Christ[1] shaped the world in ancient times.

**OIRP**

(Hail) is a cold grain,
and a shower of sleet,
and the sickness (destroyer) of snakes.

grando: hail

**LORE**

"Hail" is a complex principle which involves the projection (from "above" or "beyond") of a hard and dangerous substance which is also the "seed of becoming," new creation, and transformation — sometimes through crisis. This is clear in all the rune poems which refer to "hail" as a form of "grain" or a seed. This is

---

[1]This was probably *Hroptr* before changed by a Christian copyist.

transformation within the framework of the cosmos, and the (re-)unification of polar opposites in a productive way. Like the number nine, it represents completion.

## BRIGHT-STAVE

A change or transformation of your life situation. Perhaps crisis or trauma may be in the offing. The source of this impetus probably will come from beyond your present consciousness. Warning: Be prepared for crisis. This rune indicates self-ordering and inner harmony based on mythic models. (This is the only preparation possible.) Seek to develop pure – crystalline – ideals or principles. If change is undertaken from the impetus of crisis, a good outcome can be expected. A re-shaping of your present situation modeled on higher forms or principles (archetypes) is indicated. This rune may indicate a mystic, magician, or priest.

## MURK-STAVE

Crisis leading to destruction of your vital powers and sources of well-being is indicated. There is lack of preparation. Change for the worse. Personal stagnation is an invitation to catastrophe. Blockage of the "hail" will result in total stagnation and lack of change in life. At first, this may seem beneficial, but crisis must be controlled, not avoided entirely.

## KEYWORDS FOR *HAGALAZ*

**Bright**: Change according to ideals, Controlled crisis, Completion, Inner harmony

**Murky**: Catastrophe, Crisis, Stagnation, Loss of power

# 10.

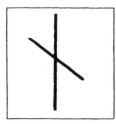

Phonetic value: N

Germanic name: *Nauthiʒ*, need, need-fire, distress

Modern English: Need

## OERP

*(Need) is constricting on the chest
although to the children of men it often becomes
a help and salvation nevertheless,
if they heed it in time.*

## ONRR

*(Need) makes for a difficult situation;
the naked freeze in the frost.*

## OIRP

*(Need) is the grief of the bondmaid,
and a hard condition to be in,
and toilsome work.*

*opera*: trouble

## LORE

"Need" is the principle of resistance or friction in the universe. As with the "hail" rune, the source of this is outside the individual's control. This is the principle of the chain of causality — cause and effect. This is a root principle of *ǫrlög* — action and reaction in a chain of events. In the darkness and cold of the need-rune the need for fire is realized, but the fire must be generated from what you have within yourself. Thus the need-fire is kindled to banish distress.

## BRIGHT-STAVE

Recognition of "need" leads to taking appropriate action to alleviate distress. Stress is turned to strength through consciousness. Resistance to the will leads to a strengthening of the will. Crisis forces original thought and self-reliance. A change leads to salvation from within the self. This rune may indicate a torrid love affair or a crisis in the present one. It also can signify a menial worker or bureaucrat—or a mystic/magician.

## MURK-STAVE

External circumstances constrain freedom. Beware a hostile environment. Your will is being resisted. The toilsome aspects of life are grinding you down. Friction is present in your inner and outer relationships. You are overly directed toward "outer" things—turn within. Blockage of the *nauthiz* leads to a lack of dynamic tension in life. There is a danger of being seduced to the "easy path" (the so-called "path of least resistance"). This would result in personal atrophy.

## KEYWORDS FOR *NAUTHIZ*

**Bright:** Resistance (leading to strength), Recognition of *ørlög*, Innovation, Need-fire (self-reliance)

**Murky:** Constraint of freedom, Distress, Toil, Drudgery, Laxity

# 11.

Phonetic value: I

Germanic name: *Isa*, ice

Modern English: Ice

## OERP

*(Ice) is very cold
and exceedingly slippery;
it glistens, clear as glass,
very much like gems,
a floor made of frost
is fair to see.*

## ONRR

*(Ice), we call the broad bridge;
the blind need to be led.*

## OIRP

*(Ice) is the rind of the river,
and the roof of the waves,
and a danger for fey men.*

*glacies*: ice

## LORE

"Ice" is the principle of absolute contraction and stasis. It gathers all things around it into itself and tries to hold them in stillness, darkness, and coldness. This is the extension of the cosmic ice of Niflheimr which balances the all-dynamism of the fires in Muspellsheimr. This force acts as a bridge between worlds due to its "solidifying" quality. It is the bonding element in the cosmos. However, in its pure state it is a destructive and dangerous element.

## BRIGHT-STAVE

Enhancement of self-consciousness and of ego awareness. Difficult situations are overcome with inner resources. Transition (not always easy) from one state of being to another. This rune may indicate a time to pull back into the self without separating from the world. You need enlightened action to guide your steps in the possible transitions. You possess self-control, the ability to influence others, unity of purpose and being. This element is not without the fascination of beauty. *Isa* also may represent a mystic, scoundrel, or dead man.

## MURK-STAVE

Out of balance, the "ice" can cause a freezing of life forces and an over-concentration in the ego center leading to dullness and stupidity. There is a danger of becoming blind to the totality. Transitions bode dangers, though the dangers may be hidden by beauty. Your will may be weakened; or, you may be controlled by others, by outside forces. A blockage of *isa* leads to a dissipation of forces and an inability to concentrate consciousness or activity.

## KEYWORDS FOR *ISA*

**Bright**: Concentrated self, (Ego) Consciousness, Self-control, Unity

**Murky**: Ego-mania, Dullness, Blindness, Dissipation

# 12.

Phonetic value: J (Y)

Germanic name: *Jera*, (good) year, harvest

Modern English: Year

## OERP

*(Harvest) is the hope of men,
when god lets,
holy king of heaven,
the earth give
her bright fruits
to the noble ones and the needy.*

## ONRR

*(Good harvest) is the profit of men;
I say that Frodhi was generous.*

## OIRP

*(Good harvest) is the profit of all men,
and a good summer,
and a ripened field.*

*annus:* year

## LORE

*Jera* is the cyclical aspect of nature, the great wheel of the year. When properly used this natural cycle yields good fruits (rewards). The year is a mechanical/organic process, not a "moral" one. This concept of eternal cycle, or eternal return, is one of the core concepts of the rune row. The other is found in the axis of the yew-rune.

BRIGHT-STAVE

Rewards for right action. Plenty and a "good harvest" can be expected. You may be the recipient of the generosity of another. Peace and tranquility born of material well-being are in the offing. You experience the organic/material manifestations of your actions. Have patience to act at the proper time. This rune may represent a farmer or someone in financial affairs.

MURK-STAVE

Enslavement to cyclical patterns. You are unable to get beyond repetitious behavior. Inappropriate timing or actions lead to negative results. Failure and poverty can result from wrong work. A blockage of the year-rune causes an inability to use cyclical, natural patterns. Ignorance of the ways of nature may lead to conflict with the self and with others as you attempt to compensate.

KEYWORDS FOR *JERA*

**Bright**: Reward, Plenty, Peace, Proper timing

**Murky**: Repetition, Bad timing, Poverty, Conflict

# 13.

Phonetic value: E, I, or EI

Germanic name: *Eihwaz*, yew

Modern English: Yew or yogh

## OERP

*(Yew) is on the outside
a rough tree
and hard, firm in the earth,
keeper of the fire,
supported by roots,
(it is a) joy on the estate.*

## ONRR

*(Yew) is the greenest wood in the winter;
there is usually, when it burns, singeing (i.e.,
it makes a hot fire).*

## OIRP

*(Yew) is a strung bow,
and brittle iron,
and Farbauti (= a giant) of the arrow.*

*arcus:* bow, rainbow

## LORE

This is the principle of the vertical axis that penetrates into the world above and the world below and connects the human realm to the heavenly and chthonic regions. It is the synthesis of above and below, light and dark, life and death. The yew is a flexible force but also hard; it endures beyond all other things.

The yew is evergreen in the winter—life in the midst of death—and it is used to build fires, thus becoming the "sun within." This is the World-Tree Yggdrasill.

## BRIGHT-STAVE

The "yew" promotes spiritual enlightenment along the vertical axis of consciousness. Mental toughness and flexibility are needed. The inner flame must be ignited through discipline. Seek independence from the natural/mechanical order of the cosmos. Controlled changes in consciousness are indicated (initiation). Realization of inner strength will protect you from outside dangers. Bring together the light and dark. This rune may also indicate a mystic or magician.

## MURK-STAVE

*Eihwaz* coming too early into the life of a person can cause deep confusion and consternation. The hot fires unconsciously ignited may cause "burn out," leading to death and decay. A stoppage of the "yew" principle in those who are prepared for it causes a profound sense of dissatisfaction, boredom, and meaninglessness. It also can soften your will and sense of self-discipline.

## KEYWORDS FOR *EIHWAZ*

**Bright**: Enlightenment, Endurance, Initiation, Protection

**Murky**: Confusion, Destruction, Dissatisfaction, Weakness

# 14.

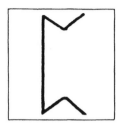

Phonetic value: P

Germanic name: *Perthro*, lot-cup, device for casting lots

Modern English: Perd

## OERP

*(Lot-box) is always*
*play and laughter*
*among bold men,*
*where the warriors sit*
*in the beer hall,*
*happily together.*

## LORE

Two things are necessary to understand the connection between the mirth described in the "beer hall" (i.e., a place where sacrificial drink is consumed) and the idea of divination or runecasting. First, you must understand that there was very little difference between the techniques and tools of runecasting and those of simple gambling. Second, you must realize that gambling was an absolute passion among the Germanic (and even Indo-European) peoples. (See the *Germania*, chapter 24.) Like war, gambling was a way to "test their luck"—which meant no less than the strength of their essential beings. This is the runic principle behind the process embodied in the three Norns— Urdhr-Verdhandi-Skuld—which results in ørlög, the ordeal of humankind. The mystery of *perthro* is what this whole book is about.

BRIGHT-STAVE

A source of joy to athlings (powerful, enlightened ones) who sit in the beer hall, i.e., a well of knowledge and ecstasy to athlings in a contemplative state contained within their psychosomatic enclosures ("hall") charged with the fluid ("beer") of Odian consciousness. This is generally a "good lot" to have, and bodes well for runecasts. It portends good fellowship and happiness, but indicates constant evolutionary change and growth. It may represent an entertainer or musician.

MURK-STAVE

Too much of this force, an addiction to its pleasures, can cause chaos, destruction, and confusion. Unwise use of *perthro* leads to dissipation and squandering of vital forces. A stoppage of this force results in stagnation, loneliness, and withering of life's pleasures.

KEYWORDS FOR *PERTHRO*

**Bright:** Good lot, Knowledge of *ørlög*, Fellowship and joy, Evolutionary change

**Murky:** Addiction, Stagnation, Loneliness, Malaise

# 15.

Phonetic value: Z

Germanic name: *Elhaz*, elk; or *algiz*, protection

Modern English: Elks

## OERP

*(Elk's) sedge has its home*
*most often in the fen,*
*it waxes in the water*
*and grimly wounds*
*and reddens ("burns") with blood*
*any man*
*who, in any way,*
*tries to grasp it.*

## LORE

This, like the *thurisaz* rune (note the thematic similarities in the OERP), is a "two-edged" concept. The OE name "elk-sedge" is a kenning, or poetic name, for sword. Essentially, *elhaz* is the principle of numinous attraction and even union between the individual consciousness and the "higher self" embodied in the fetch of *fylgja*. (See *Runelore*, chapter 8.) This contact, of course, can be dangerous when attempted by one who is unprepared. As with the *eihwaz* rune, this also may be put into arboreal symbology to show the connection between the "roots and branches" of anything. Or it may take the shape of the "Rainbow Bridge" (Bifröst) which connects the human mind with the grandeur of the gods.

BRIGHT-STAVE

Except for the experienced athling or runester, this runestave can bode danger. For those who know not to "grasp" the *elhaz* but to "become" it, however, divine realizations await. Do not barge in like a warrior, but rather approach with the craft of an Odian. This craft or awakening is foreshadowed. Divine communcation is indicated. Also, this force can be turned around and used in an attack or to protect yourself. Generally this rune does not signify persons, but rather divine forces.

MURK-STAVE

Grave dangers lie hidden. Lack of preparedness leads to being consumed by awesome, archetypal forces and can result in injury to the self. Blockage of this force may be a blessing to most people. For athlings or Erulians, however, it means being cut off from an important well-spring of inspiration – the fetch (Greek *daimon*, Latin *genius*).

KEYWORDS FOR *ELHAZ*

**Bright**: Connection with the gods, Awakening, Higher life, Protection

**Murky**: Hidden danger, Consumption by divine forces, Loss of divine link

# 16.

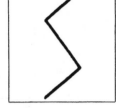

Phonetic value: S

Germanic name: *Sowilo*, sun

Modern English: Sun

OERP

*(Sun) is by sea-men
always hoped for
when they fare far away
over the fishes bath
until the brine-stallion
they bring to land.*

ONRR

*(Sun) is the light of the lands;
I bow to the holyness.*

OIRP

*(Sun) is the shield of the clouds,
and a shining glory,
and the life-long sorrow (= destroyer) of ice.*

*rota:* wheel

LORE

This is the principle of the guide. It is also the goal after which the runester quests. It shines like a beacon attracting and encouraging those who seek it. *Sowilo* is the sun-wheel; it not only guides but also is itself a dynamically moving, spinning symbol, a counter-balance to the *isa*-rune. This is the rune of higher being. The S-rune is also a sign of the often ignored serpentine mysteries of the North which show the necessity of dealing with darkness to win true wisdom (see Ódhinn's rewinning of the poetic mead, *Runelore*, chapter 9).

## BRIGHT-STAVE

There is reason for hope. Good guidance is being given. If you are "lost" you will find your way. Fixed concentration on your goal leads to success. This rune bodes well for any journey, especially those over water. Listen to higher rede (= counsel) from within the self or from others. The light of the "sun" burns away all external appearances ("ice"), leaving only the essential reality. This force will protect the runester from hostile powers. It will break cosmic or psychological inertia and help the journey along. *Sowilo* brings honor and luck. Educational undertakings may be in the offing. This rune also may signify a sailor or a teacher.

## MURK-STAVE

Bad counsel. This rune reveals an unthinking attraction to, and pursuit of, goals set by others. False success is gained by dishonorable means. There is a tendency to look outside yourself for answers to questions and for guidance. Gullibility. Blockage of the "sun" leads to loss of your sense of purpose and goals in life. Confusion and eventual defeat of your plans are due to a lack of direction.

## KEYWORDS FOR *SOWILO*

**Bright**: Guidance, Hope, Success, Goals achieved, Honor

**Murky**: False goals, Bad counsel, False success, Gullibility, Loss of goals

## 17.

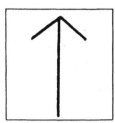

Phonetic value: T

Germanic name: *Tiwaz*, the god Tiw (Týr)

Modern English: Teu

OERP

*(Tir) is a star,*
*it keeps faith well*
*with athlings,*
*always on its course*
*over the mists of night*
*it never fails.*

ONRR

*(Týr) is the one-handed among the AEsir;*
*the smith has to blow often.*

OIRP

*(Týr) is the one-handed god,*
*and the leavings of the wolf,*
*and the ruler of the temple.*

Mars: Mars

LORE

This rune is a three-fold principle of (1) order (justice, law), (2) self-sacrifice, and (3) the world column. Each of these really derives from the unified principle of independent ordered existence, whose servants will sacrifice themselves for its sake. Its main cosmic function is the separation of the heavens and earth by the world column (Irminsūl) so that manifestation can take place in the "created" space. *Tiwaz* is the sign of the "pole-" or "load-star" used as a constant guide through the night sky.

## BRIGHT-STAVE

This is the lot of *troth* (faith, loyalty) and trust that endures in the face of all hardships. Justice can be expected, and good judgment based on a careful analysis of the facts. Victory will be yours if you have acted wisely. Strive to order the environment in a rational way. The path to success may lie through self-sacrifice. Vigilance and hard work combined with knowledge are necessary. Reliability, loyalty, faithfulness must be practiced, and can be expected. Strive for exactitude and precision, plan very carefully. Make your work methodical. Analytical models based on mathematical principles are indicated. The rune may indicate a scientist or academic.

## MURK-STAVE

You have a tendency to become bogged down in analysis and details, which may lead to a paralysis of action and a limitation in vision. You are always planning, never doing. Self-sacrifice is to the detriment of the ultimate interests—"sacrificing over-much." A stoppage of *tiwaz* force leads to injustice, imbalance, confusion, a deterioration of rationality.

## KEYWORDS FOR *TIWAZ*

**Bright**: Troth, Justice, Rationality, Self-sacrifice, Analysis

**Murky**: Mental paralysis, Over-analysis, Over-sacrifice, Injustice, Imbalance

# 18.

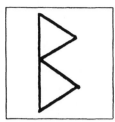

Phonetic value: B

Germanic name: *Berkano*, birch, the birch goddess or twig

Modern English: Birch

## OERP

*(Birch) is without fruit
but just the same it bears
limbs without fertile seed;
it has beautiful branches,
high on its crown
it is finely covered,
loaded with leaves,
touching the sky.*

## ONRR

*(Birch-twig) is the limb greenest with leaves,
Loki brought the luck of deceit.*

## OIRP

*(Birch-twig) is a leafy limb,
and a little tree,
and a youthful wood.*

*abies:* silver fir

## LORE

The *berkano* principle is one of self-contained and continuous propagation or growth. It is the principle of birth itself which is never "born" but always is. This lot expands itself without losing its self-consciousness. It is a creative originator of being that extends into the heavens and into the nether regions. The B-rune is a collector and conserver of energy and a sign of enclosure and shelter. The birch is the liberator of pent-up energies, which when released lead to new growth.

## BRIGHT-STAVE

New beginnings based on old patterns are indicated. Gradual changes are on the way. Look for the importance of new things, things that might seem small at their birth. Spiritual growth comes within tradition. Domestic change occurs within a tranquil environment. New aspects are introduced into erotic relationships. Prosperity and beauty are indicated. Some elements of craft, deceit, or viciousness may be necessary to achieve goals. This rune may represent a mother or a whore.

## MURK-STAVE

Submersion into the "natural world" leads to a blurring of self-consciousness and awareness. There is a fascination with the sheer beauty of the world of appearances. Deceit is a danger. A blockage of the "birch" can lead to sterility of mind and body, and stagnation in all aspects of life.

## KEYWORDS FOR *BERKANO*

**Bright**: Birth, Becoming, Life changes, Shelter, Liberation

**Murky**: Blurring of consciousness, Deceit, Sterility, Stagnation

# 19.

Phonetic value: E

Germanic name: *Ehwaz*, (war) horse; or *ehwo*, the two horses

Modern English: Eh

## OERP

ᛗ (Horse) is, in front of the earls
the joy of athlings,
a charger proud on its hooves;
when concerning it, heroes —
wealthy men — on war-horses
exchange speech,
and it is always a comfort
to the restless.

## LORE

This is the principle of "teamwork," especially in tandem. It represents two different, yet harmoniously working entities. In traditional Germanic culture this is most clearly experienced in the special relationship between rider (*mannaz*) and horse (*elhaz*), or by observing how a team of horses works. This is, then, a metaphor for the relationship of the self to the body and/or the special inner bond between any two entities or things that are directed toward noble endeavors.

## BRIGHT-STAVE

Dynamic harmony with others is indicated, especially with a partner, mentor, husband, or wife. There is teamwork without loss of individuality. You understand the necessity of give and take, and accept unique differences in the other. Good results are indicated. Develop a relationship with your fetch. Marriage or other formal partnership may be in the offing. Mutual trust and loyalty are necessary and present. The rune may represent your spouse or partner in some endeavor.

## MURK-STAVE

Loss of self in the partner is indicated. Too much "harmony" leads to sameness and duplication of efforts. A stoppage of the *ehwaz* results in mistrust, betrayal, disharmony, divorce.

## KEYWORDS FOR *EHWAZ*

**Bright**: Harmony, Teamwork, Trust, Loyalty

**Murky**: Duplication, Disharmony, Mistrust, Betrayal

# 20.

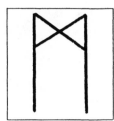

Phonetic value: M

Germanic name: *Mannaz*, human being

Modern English: Man

## OERP

*(Man) is in his mirth*
*dear to his kinsman;*
*although each shall*
*depart from the other;*
*for the lord wants to commit,*
*by his decree,*
*that frail flesh*
*to the earth.*

## ONRR

*(Man) is the increase of dust;*
*mighty is the talon-span of the hawk.*

## OIRP

*(Man) is the joy of man,*
*and the increase of dust,*
*and the adornment of ships.*

*homo:* human

## LORE

"Man" is the principle of embodied self-consciousness. This symbolizes humankind's earthly life as a heroic struggle, and points to the reality that we are only truly human when in the flesh. The stave refers to the origin of humanity (both Askr and Embla) as a result of the three-fold gift of Ódhinn-Vili-Vé, and to the origin of three-fold human society (farmers, fighters and rulers/magicians). Both myths show the shaping of people on earth (Midhgardhr) in the image of the divine—both in consciousness and in order. Our mortality—as that of the gods—ensures becoming.

## BRIGHT-STAVE

This is the lot of humanity, of humanness with all its great nobility and power of spirit, as well as its weakness and mortality. Great intelligence born of divine or higher knowledge is indicated. Individuation of the self is needed. There is happiness in inner and social life, born of a realization of the truths of human existence. Blinders will be removed; you will see things as they are. Awakening. This rune could indicate any person, but especially seekers of all kinds.

## MURK-STAVE

Depression due to a perception of hopelessness is indicated. You dwell on mortality and weakness, fearing true knowledge. Relationships are based on lies and misperceptions. A blockage of *mannaz* leads to blindness, self-delusion, and a tendency to live in a fantasy world.

## KEYWORDS FOR *MANNAZ*

**Bright**: Divine structure, Intelligence, Awareness, Social order

**Murky**: Depression, Mortality, Blindness, Self-delusion

# 21.

Phonetic value: L

Germanic name: *Laguz*, water, lake; or *laukaz*, leek

Modern English: Lake or leek

## OERP

*(Water) is to people*
*seemingly unending*
*if they should venture out*
*on an unsteady ship*
*and the sea waves*
*frighten them very much,*
*and the brine-stallion*
*does not heed its bridle.*

## ONRR

*(Water) is (that), which falls from the mountain;*
*as a force; but gold (objects) are costly things.*

## OIRP

*(Wetness) is churning water,*
*and a wide kettle,*
*and the land of fish.*

*lacus*: lake

## LORE

This is the principle of cosmic water welling up from Niflheimr and containing the potential for life. This water is the great sea of dynamic forces into which you are thrust during your voyage of becoming. The deep can represent that vast sea of the world of which humankind is usually unconscious, and which can be threatening if you are voyaging in a "vessel" that is subject to disturbances on this "sea." A "downward" flow of vital energy is indicated. The alternate name "leek" indicates growth upward.

## BRIGHT-STAVE

Stern tests in life are indicated, but you have the vital energies to stand these tests. The self evolves through the experience of true initiation. Transition from one state of being to another. Begin at once to act. Control of the self is most needed. Do not fear the journey. By "going under" you will gain the gold of well-being. Personal growth will occur through perhaps uncomfortable situations. A sailor, fisherman, or lawyer may be represented by this rune.

## MURK-STAVE

Fear of change, fear of the journey and of the unknown vastness within the deep self are present. There is a danger of "going around in circles," avoiding the path, avoiding life. Failing the test is indicated. A stoppage of *laguz* dams up the vital force and leads to stunted growth, withering, and poverty. Access to the deep self is blocked.

## KEYWORDS FOR *LAGUZ*

**Bright**: Life, "Water" journey, Sea of vitality, Sea of unconscious, Growth

**Murky**: Fear, Circular motion, Avoidance, Withering

# 22.

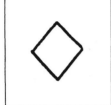

Phonetic value: NG

Germanic name: *Ingwaz*, the god Ing

Modern English: Ing

## OERP

*(Ing) was first, among the East-Danes,*
*seen by men*
*until he again eastward (or "back")*
*went over the wave;*
*the wain followed on;*
*this is what the warriors*
*called the hero.*

## LORE

This is the principle of contained, isolated separation, which is absolutely necessary to any transformational process. "Ing" is the stasis of being which forms a step along the path of eternal becoming. Entering into this principle is a movement "widdershins" – against the sun – "to the east" into the realm of darkness inhabited by the etins (giants). In this realm of darkness and solitude new growth arises.

## BRIGHT-STAVE

"Ing" is the stave of rest, of active internal growth. There is a deep-level gestation of new power. Rest, let things "gestate," to be brought forth at the right time in full maturity. Have patience. Listen to yourself. This lot indicates concepts or aspects that have had the benefit of such a period of gestation. This is a time of stasis to be followed by fertile dynamism. Things are in a potential state awaiting activation. This rune may signify a farmer or a priest.

## MURK-STAVE

The misapplication of "ing" can lead to self-absorption and to a disassociation from the environment. You can become "bottled up" in the subjective world, unable to interact with objectivity. Paralytic stasis is indicated. This can be a seductive force, fooling you into thinking it is the "end" rather than a stage; thus it is the curse of many mystics. On the other hand, a blockage of the NG-stave can lead to a scattering of essence or a sense of meaningless motion — without stages at which essence can be gathered and consolidated. There is movement but without real change, and unbridled dynamism.

## KEYWORDS FOR *INGWAZ*

**Bright**: Rest stage, Internal growth, Gestation

**Murky**: Impotence, Scattering, Movement without change

# 23.

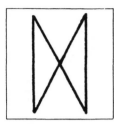

Phonetic value: D

Germanic name: *Dagaz*, day

Modern English: Day

OERP

*(Day) is the lord's messenger,*
*dear to men,*
*the ruler's famous light;*
*(it is) mirth and hope*
*to rich and poor*
*(and) is useful for all.*

## LORE

This is the ultimate principle of bipolar creativity. It is a unique stave of consciousness as a developed, evolved form of the gifts of the god(s) Ódhinn-Vili-Vé. In the light of day all seemingly polar opposites are brought together and understood. This is the rune of enlightened consciousness.

## BRIGHT-STAVE

"Day" brings the boon of archetypal awareness, which can sometimes seem spontaneous. It is a source—really the only true source—of hope and happiness. The power of "day" can be known to all who seek it earnestly. A great awakening is at hand. True vision will be gained. This light may be found where you do not expect it. Seek the ideal. "Day" represents a true seeker.

MURK-STAVE

It is difficult for "day" to be seen as a murk-stave in the active sense. The only detriment would be its manifestation in the life of someone who did not want or who was not prepared for it. Of course, a blockage of the light of "day" means blindness, dullness, boredom, hopelessness, etc.

KEYWORDS FOR *DAGAZ*

**Bright**: Awakening, Awareness, Hope/happiness, The ideal

**Murky**: Blindness, Hopelessness

# 24.

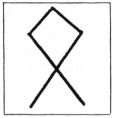

Phonetic value: O

Germanic name: *Othala*, ancestral property-

Modern English: Odal

## OERP

(Estate) is very dear
to every man,
if he can enjoy what is right
and according to custom
in his dwelling,
most often in prosperity

## LORE

This is the principle of the "homeland" in its most ideal form. It represents the "inside" vs. the "outside." Psychologically, it is the self in all its complexity as distinguished from non-self. Socially, it is the group (be it family, clan, tribe, guild, order, etc.) distinguished from those outside that group. Right order must be preserved in this group for it to work. Although secure in the home, there is continued interaction—give and take—with the environment. It is the "home within," i.e., the ideal reality which is not attached to any particular "land." *Othala* is complete freedom. It is the active consolidation of all gains.

## BRIGHT-STAVE

"Odal" is the lot of stable prosperity and well-being. A solid and peaceful home-, family-, or group-life is indicated, and one that leads to continued growth. Attention must always be paid to customs and order within the group and to the vigilant defense of the group. There is true freedom stemming from a secure base. A new dwelling or a new allegiance may be in the offing. Productive interaction with "outsiders" is a continuing possibility. This lot may indicate a leader of some kind, or a whole group of people.

## MURK-STAVE

Again this stave is difficult to see in an actively negative way. The only danger comes through not preserving right customary or traditional order within a group, thus limiting the powers of leaders. A misunderstanding of "odal" can lead to a totalitarianism that runs counter to the interests of the whole. All of this will lead to disaster. A stoppage of the O-stave, however, will end in slavery to outside forces, poverty, homelessness, and loneliness.

## KEYWORDS FOR OTHALA

**Bright**: A home, Group prosperity, Group order, Freedom, Productive interaction

**Murky**: Lack of customary order, Totalitarianism, Slavery, Poverty, Homelessness

# 4

# The Tools of Runecasting

AS A METHOD OF DIVINATION, runecasting is remarkably flexible in the ways it can be used. Theoretically, all you need are twenty-four slips of paper on which the stave shapes could be written, for the magic is in the self of the runester, not in the objects. However, for most runesters a permanent set of runestaves and a set of special runecasting tools are essential for maintaining the all-important sense of connection, dedication, and intensity.

The physical objects upon which the staves are carved may be left up to the runester. The "staves" can be made of wood, bone, stone, earthenware, or another material you like, and in whatever size and shape you prefer. The only thing I strongly urge is that you make your own runestaves. I suggested this for two reasons: (1) the runestaves are so simple anyone can easily make them (so take advantage of what is traditional), and (2) from a magical and talismanic viewpoint even slips of paper marked with a ballpoint pen are superior to mass-produced "rune cookies" since you put your own energy into the runestaves as you make them. This being said, it is still better to start working with quality manufactured staves than to put off too long the beginnings of actual work.

What kind of staves (or even "cards") the runester eventually will want to work with is largely a matter of taste or personal preference. I suggest a period of experimentation; see in practice which kind you prefer. In actual use, this may be different than what you preferred in theory.

There are several types of runestaves: (1) small and round (of pottery, wood, or bone), (2) small rectangular slips of wood, (3) short, or (4) long rune tines, and even (5) cards. Examples of each of these types are illustrated in figure 4.1, shown in their approximately actual sizes.

Although different kinds of runestaves may be more suitable for certain types of castings or layings, really any kind of stave can be used effectively for almost any method.

The small round stave may be made from tree branches (or even dowels) about one-half to three-fourths of an inch in diameter cut at intervals of about one-fourth of an inch. The result is

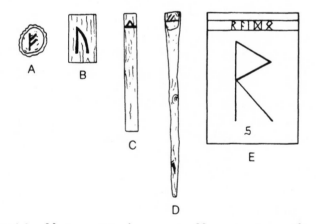

Figure 4.1. Various types of runestaves. Here we see examples of A) small round runestave—this one is of wood; B) runestave made of a small rectangular piece of wood; C) short and D) long runestave; and E) a "card" runestave.

a set of small disks on which you can carve the runestaves. This general type also can be fashioned from wooden beads—but spherical shapes can roll and thus prove unsuitable for some methods of runecasting.

Small rectangular wooden slips can be made from carefully shaven and trimmed strips of wood, about one-sixteenth of an inch thick. This is probably the type Tacitus was describing. But they also can be fashioned from thin sheets of wood veneer. (These veneer sheets can be obtained in most hardware or hobby shops.)

Shorter runelots or rune tines may be fashioned from short lengths (two to three inches) of twigs or from square strips of hardwood (about one-quarter inch wide). This kind and the rectangular wooden slips are most convenient for carrying in your pocket or purse.

The longer runestaves are perhaps the most traditional forms. Although no such examples have ever been found, ancient written descriptions seem to point in this direction. This type of runestave can be made easily from tapering twigs five to six inches long and one-quarter to one-half an inch wide at the top. They can be left rough, the bark still on them, with only a small surface smoothed at the large end on which the runestave can be carved.

Finally, for methods of divination that require laying out runic patterns, cards also can be fashioned. To these you might want to add information, such as the rune name or its numerical value, that could be helpful in your rune readings. These can be made easily from posterboard or blank paper cards of a size and shape that is pleasing to you.

The actual materials used in the creation of the runestaves can be of some importance. For the lots or staves themselves, organic substances, such as wood or bone, are preferred. Wood is, of course, the most traditional and the most widely used material for this purpose, but bone and even precious metals perhaps were also used for divination. The symbolism of the use of wood is clear in the Germanic cultural context. It reminds us of the World-Tree, Yggdrasill, at the roots of which lies the Well of Wyrd, and in whose roots and branches the runestaves shimmer as a mighty web-work. Use your intuition to decide what species of wood is best suited for your runestaves. Tacitus reports that fruit- or nut-bearing trees were used, but it is perhaps more important that you choose a wood that has special value or meaning to you. It is also possible to make the staves out of various kinds of wood, each one corresponding to the runestave carved upon it. The runester is urged to make use of intuition, but you also may want to consult Table A, column X in *Futhark*.[1]

The runestaves also will be colored. The traditional paint or dye used for this can be made easily from red ochre. (Other natural red pigments are also good.) Of course, the substance originally used was blood, but even in prehistoric times red ochre was being used as a substitute for blood. However, different colors—as determined by intuition—are also possible. White, however, as a color for the staves themselves, should be avoided since the cloth on which they will be cast is white.

One of the wonderful things about runecasting is that you can be as traditional or an innovative as you wish. It is relatively simple to include traditional elements with innovative techniques. For the ritual elements of the traditional shaping of rune-lots, see chapter 5.

The cloth upon which the lots are cast should be made of white material. Not only does Tacitus indicate this in his report, but this practice is borne out by the symbolism of white as a sign of the undifferentiated sum of magical light. It is upon this white field that the runes play out their interweavings of force. The cloth itself should be made of linen or some other natural material, and should be between three and four feet square.

Some runesters decorate their cloths in meaningful ways. If you refer to chapter 6 you will see methods of runecasting that

---

[1]Edred Thorsson, *Futhark: A Handbook of Rune Magic* (York Beach, ME: Samuel Weiser, 1984): 147.

call for the runester to read certain significances into various fields on the cloth (see figure 6.9). This pattern could be stitched onto the cloth if the runester wanted, or it simply could be envisioned with the *hugauga*—the magical eye. If the runester uses such lines on the cloth, they should be of dark blue or black and be as thin as possible. This latter point is merely a practical one for ease in making readings.

When not in use, the runestaves or runelots should be stored in a suitable container. A cloth or leather bag or a wooden box is ideal for this. Such a container is of the greatest importance if you have shaped and loaded your runelots as "talismanic creatures" with their own *ørlög*.

Some runesters like to cast their runelots from a lot cup (the wooden box can also serve this purpose). The lot cup can be made of horn, leather, or wood and can be any shape the runester determines. The only important factor is that it is large enough to hold all twenty-four lots easily and loosely. This cup, should it be treated as a *taufr* (talisman) itself, should be loaded with the *perthro* rune.

In very formal rites of runecasting, especially those of cosmic significance carried out by true Erulians, a three-legged stool painted gold is also needed. (This, however, is not necessary for most runecasters' purposes.) The runester sits upon this stool, called "theal's stool," before beginning to formulate a reading.

Other tools and equipment as needed in general runework are described more fully in *Futhark*.[2]

---

[2]Edred Thorsson, *Futhark: A Handbook of Rune Magic* (York Beach, ME: Samuel Weiser, 1984): 83–89.

# 5

# Rites of Runecasting

THE USE OF RITUAL IN every operation of runecasting is important for two reasons: to avoid the "parlor game" attitude that sometimes envelopes such sacred activity, and to help the runester reach a state of concentrated consciousness that will improve the quality of the casting and reading. Ritual work will put the runester in an altered state of mind that will direct his or her concentration to the question at hand, or to the general life situation of greatest importance at that time – thus opening the doors of communication between the runecaster and the realm of the norns. After some time has been spent working with runecasting, the vitki will begin to feel that in certain operations he or she was more "in sync" than in others. To ensure this state on a regular basis is the function of inner ritual work.

Although the runester is free to create such ritual formulas as he or she sees fit, I urge everyone to carry out faithfully the example formulas a few times to see if the traditional methods are right for you. It is a great misfortune that the old Germanic tradition has been so neglected—especially since we have descriptions of the exact methods used for many centuries. After consulting all the traditional sources, the following complex ritual formula appears to have existed from the most ancient times:

1) Cutting and scoring of staves

2) Calling on the norns (or other gods and entities)

3) Casting the staves (onto the white cloth)

4) Calling on the gods (or other entities)

5) Choosing staves (in threes or multiples of three)

6) Sitting on the theal's stool

7) Reading of the staves

8) Confirmation by omens, etc.

This would represent a complex and elaborate kind of runecasting, but elements from this great formula should be kept in mind as bases for experimentation.

# Time

The season and the time of day the runester chooses to undertake runecastings, especially important castings, deserve some thought. Traditionally the runester takes into account (1) season (position of the sun in the yearly cycle), (2) moon phase, and (3) time of day (position of the sun in the daily cycle). Of course, the time chosen should conform to the kind of reading being undertaken, or the nature of the question. Inquiries involving new beginnings perhaps would be carried out most effectively at times associated with beginnings, during the yuletide for example (about December 21-January 2), at (Easter[1] or Ostara – the springtime festival at or around the spring equinox), nights just after the new moon, or just before the full moon at sunrise. The first three nights after the new moon, the fifth, seventh, eighth, ninth, twelfth, nineteenth, twentieth, twenty-third, and twenty-sixth nights of the moon are well suited to divinatory work, too. To find the correct night (or "day"),[2] count from the first night of the new moon. There are, of course, twenty-eight nights in the lunar cycle. Also, for consulting the runes on inner or eso-teric matters, nighttime is preferred, while on exoteric or other mundane affairs the daylight hours are best.

It should be remembered also that these times are merely optimal ritual aids; from a fully Odian viewpoint they can be dispensed with.

# Stead

For practical reasons, most runecasting will probably be carried out indoors, in your living quarters. For ritual effectiveness other runework should be done in the same area. One advan-tage to runecasting is that the vitki can carry the basic "holy stead" around in the form of the white cloth. However, for especially important castings other holy steads might also be considered. Most beneficial are sites under holy trees – oaks, beeches, yews, ashes – or near (south of if possible) a natural spring or an artificial well. Hilltops are also good places to do runework. Outdoors, the runecaster can follow the rede of the ancient tradition more effectively and look into the sky when picking the staves for the reading. The force can be especially

---

[1]The term Easter, or *Eostre*, was adopted by the Christians from the already existing name of the Germanic goddess. The Germanic peoples' spring festival celebrated the resurrection of the White Krist.

[2]The ancient Germanic peoples counted by nights, not days.

powerful at night if you look directly to the Northern Star—into the eye of Ódhinn—while choosing the lots.

# Talismanic Creation of Lots

The physical objects or media upon which the runic characters are executed are referred to by various terms: staves (ON *stafir*), tines (ON *teinar*), or lots (ON *hlautar*), but all are *taufar*, talismans. Ideally, each runestave should be shaped and loaded according to the principles of talismanic creation outlined in *Futhark* (pp. 108-116). At the very least, the runester can concentrate upon the name and value of the rune as he or she draws it on a slip of cardboard in red ink—which can result in effective runestaves. However, for those who want to shape twenty-four mighty rune tines, each loaded with the living power to interact directly with the norns, with the All-Father, and with all the forces within the runester, a more formal path is needed.

## CUTTING WOOD FOR LOTS

If the vitki wishes to cut his or her own staves from a living tree, certain ritual procedures might be followed. Once a tree has been selected (one tree or many can be used for shaping the twenty-four lots), the runester should go to the tree in a working attitude at dawn, noon, twilight, or midnight to cut the lot(s). The time chosen will be determined by the character of the rune lot to be cut. Find a branch bending to the *ætt* or airt of heaven that corresponds to the rune in question. (More about this in chapter 6, figure 6.8.) However, before cutting the lot, perform the Hammer Rite (see below and *Futhark*, pp. 91-93) or a similar hallowing rite in which the whole tree (roots and branches) is enveloped in the working sphere. Then position yourself close to the branch or twig you intend to cut. You may have to climb the tree to do this, of course. Turn your mind to the might and to the might of the tree, and speak the *formáli*:

> Hail to thee, might of (tree name, e.g., "oak")!
> I bid thee give this branch!
> Into it send thy speed,
> to it bind the might of the rune of (rune name, e.g.,
>    *fehu*)!

Now cut the part of the branch you want while humming or singing the name of the rune.

Once the raw material for the lot has been removed, the runester should give thanks to the wight of the tree for its gift:

> Wight of the (tree name), take my thanks.
> Henceforth be thy might in this branch!
> Deeply bound to the rune of (rune name).

This ritual procedure can be adapted for cutting one large branch from which all twenty-four lots will be shaped simply by invoking all the rune names. Also, the rite can be modified to accommodate other raw forms such as stone, metal, bone, etc.


## LOADING THE RUNELOTS

With the following procedure the runester will shape non-specific talismans loaded with the simple essence of a single rune. This can be done on twenty-four separate days, one lot each day. Or, groups (e.g., of the *ættir*) of runes can be loaded together, or the whole futhark of twenty-four runes can be done at one time. The lot(s) should already be prepared with smooth surfaces to receive the carvings. The runester will need a suitable setting with an altar or bench of some kind, a ritual knife or carving tool, equipment for staining the runestave (pigment and a pointed stave or a brush), and whatever other ritual attire or equipment is deemed necessary.

Go to the stead of working at the right tide and begin the rite.

**Opening:** This is best done with a form of the Hammer Rite to hallow the stead and ward it against unwanted things.

1) Facing north, raise your right index finger and begin with *fehu* in the north. Visualize a bright red light being projected from the tip of your finger. With this light trace the runes of the futhark standing in a ring around you about five to six feet away from your body. Draw each rune about one foot high. Turn in a clockwise direction and trace each rune so that the circle ends with *othala* in the north next to *fehu*. As you draw each rune in the air intone its name.

2) Again, facing north, stand with your arms straight out and visualize an equilateral cross lying horizontally in the plane of the rune ring with your solar plexus as the center of the cross. The arms of this cross end at the points where they intersect the rune band in the north, south, east, and west. Imagine a surrounding sphere of shimmering blue light which has the red band as its equator. Now, visualize a vertical axis coming through the length of your body from infinite space above and infinite space below. Feel and see the force flowing into your solar plexus from all six fields as it builds a ball of glowing red might at your center.

3) Now, touch your right index finger to your solar plexus, and gathering some of the rune might in your hand, thrust it forward, sending the force from that center to a point on the inside face of the outer sphere. Then sign the hammer ⊥ with the

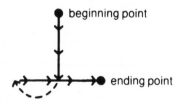

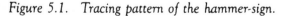

*Figure 5.1. Tracing pattern of the hammer-sign.*

collected magical might. The sign should be traced as in figure 5.1. As this is done, intone the words:

"Hammer in the North, hallow and hold this holy stead!"[3]

Then turning 90° to the right, trace another hammer sign, saying:

"Hammer in the East, hallow and hold this holy stead!"

And in the south:

"Hammer in the South, hallow and hold this holy stead!"

And in the west:

"Hammer in the West, hallow and hold this holy stead!"

Returning to the north, direct your gaze upward; there again trace the sign of the hammer on the "ceiling" of the sphere, saying:

"Hammer over me, hallow and hold this holy stead!"

And then project the hammer sign below to the "floor" of the sphere (not the ground or floor of the room) and intone:

"Hammer below me, hallow and hold this holy stead!"

Now, strike the "cross" position with your arms straight out and say:

"Hammer hallow and hold this holy stead!"

---

[3]For an old Norse version, see Edred Thorsson, *Futhark: A Hardbook of Esoteric Runology* (York Beach, ME: Samuel Weiser, 1984): 91-92.

Turning to the right, repeat this once for each of the other four (or eight) directions and once for the vertical axis.

4) Finally, center the forces by folding your arms in from the cross position with your fingers touching at the solar plexus and say:

"Around me and in me, Ásgardhr and Midhgardhr!"

**Preparation of Dye (optional):** If the pigment (e.g., ochre and linseed oil) has not already been prepared, the runester may ritually grind it at this time. Sit facing the harrow (and altar) in the north, grind the pigment with the oil and sing:

Blood of Kvasir
be now blessed,
runemight blooms in the blend!

**Preliminary Galdar:** Standing before the harrow in the *elhaz*-rune position (with arms stretched up at a 45° angle), call upon the name(s) of the rune(s) you intend to load. Repeat the name(s), this time tracing the rune(s) with your finger (or *gandr*) over the raw lot(s). Repeat the name(s) a third time while you stand in the *elhaz*-rune position. This prepares the staves for their runic leading.

**Risting (carving):** Sitting or standing before the harrow, carve the stave form into the lot while singing the rune name (or the full *galdr* of the rune). Of course, only one runestave will be carved on each lot. During this process feel, see, and concentrate on the shining runemight as it willfully flows from the heavens, earth, and subterranean realms through your center, through your arm and knife or rister, into the substance of the lot. Visualize the runemight being inlaid into the grooves made by your knife.

**Coloring (reddening):** Take up the container of stain and using a thin tool (a specially pointed stave is ideal for this; see *Futhark*, p. 87) or a thin brush inlay the grooves of the runestave with the vivifying substance. Again sing the rune name or *galdr* while thinking of the deep meaning of the mystery. After the coloring has been completed, you may want to spend some time meditating on the whole rune on all its levels of meaning.

**Loading (*formáli*):** As a final way of setting the "doom" of the lot, to speak its *ørlög* if you will, a poetic *formáli* should be spoken over it. This could be one of the old traditional verses from one of the rune poems, or a special verse of your own making. This, or some other similar formula, also can act as a mnemonic in actual rune readings.

**Holding:** To bind the might of the rune to the lot, trace three rings around the *taufr* (talisman) while singing:

> Runemight hold
> the holy runes,
> right rede shall
> they ever rown. ("rown" = whisper)

**Closing:** After placing the lot in its storage container (box, cloth, etc.), sing a short closing verse:

> Now the work
> has been wrought
> with the might
> of mikle runes,
> so shall it be!

## RUNECASTING

Not every runecasting or laying needs to be carried out with the great solemnity of the working which follows. However, the more important the question, the more ritual the true runester will want to use. In a way, the ritual can be seen as a kind of "magical overkill"; the more ways in which communicative links between the inner and outer realms are forged, the more chance there is of gaining that special sense of "rightness," of being "in sync." From the traditional standpoint, such workings are seen as no less fundamental than the cast itself; it is a whole operation.

**Preparation:** For a full ritual runecasting the white cloth should be laid out before the harrow (if one is used) with one flat side to the north. Depending on the type of cast or layout being done, the theal's stool (if one is used) should either be to the south of the cloth, or to the north of it in front of the altar or harrow as shown in figure 5.2.

**Opening:** Perform a Hammer Rite of the kind described in the lot-carving working above.

**Call to the norns:** Facing north, in the *elhaz*-rune position, call out to the power of the norns to help you cast and read the runes:

> Out of homes all-hidden
> out of the ways all-wide,
> need be I name the norns,
> and deem the dises draw neigh.
> [Pause]
> Urdhr-Verdhandi-Skuld.

With this verse the runester concentrates on engaging the "nornic forces" on two levels: (1) the personal norns (with whose "help" the runic streams can be engaged), the (2) the Great Norns—as the impersonal dynamic matrix of constant change.

**Question:** Now concentrate for a period in silence on the question at hand. While doing this, shuffle the staves in your hands or shake them in the box or cup. Once it is felt that a firm link

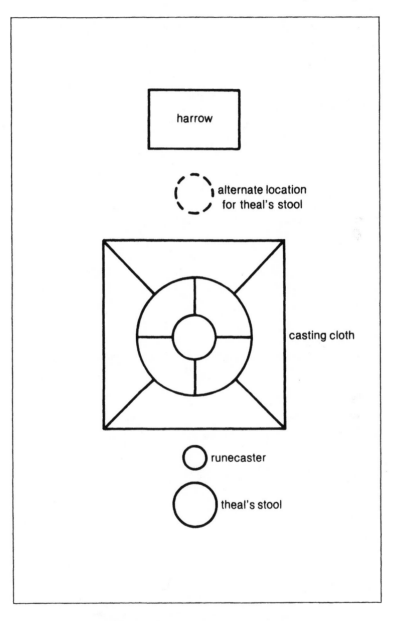

*Figure 5.2. Configuration of elements of runecasting ritual.*

between the nornic forces and the question has been forged, repeat the formula silently or aloud.

Rúnar rádh rétt rádh!
> or

Runes rown right rede!

**Casting:** Now, while gazing upward (to the Northern Star if you are outdoors) cast the runelots upon the white cloth spread out before you. As the lots are in the air, call out:

Urdhr-Verdhandi-Skuld!

Note: If a rune-laying [and not a rune-casting] method is being used, questioning and casting are combined in such a way that while the lots or cards are shuffled or otherwise randomized, the question is being posed mentally. The process is then concluded with the "Runes rown right rede" and "Urdhr-Verdhandi-Skuld" formulas.

**Call to Ódhinn:** After the lots have landed, and while still gazing aloft, the runester strikes the *elhaz*-posture and says:

Ódhinn open my eye
that I may see the staves
and read the runes aright.
[Pause]
Ódhinn-Vili-Vé!

With this verse you engage your abilities to choose the staves with inner vision. (Note: Some may wish to substitute a verse to Frigga here.)

**Choosing:** (Skip this step if you are using a pure casting method in which the lots are read as they lie on the white cloth.) Now, with your eyes still directed upward, kneel down and blindly pick the right number of lots for the method being employed. It is, of course, very important to be sure to keep the lots in the proper order as chosen from the cloth. Lay them aside carefully — one at a time as you choose them. (Note: If a laying method is being used, the lots or cards should be laid out in their proper configuration at this time.)

**Reading:** If a theal's stool or chair is being used, the runecaster should sit down upon it now — still facing north — and lay the lots out in their right order according to the method being used, either on the harrow or on the edge of the white cloth. If a reading is to be made directly from the lay of the lots on the cloth, position the theal's stool to the south of the cloth and examine the configurations. Settle your mind at this stage, and before beginning the reading (especially when reading for others), intone this verse based on "Hávamál," st. 111:

> Time is come to sing
> upon the stool of the theal
> at the well of wyrd:
>
> I saw but said naught
> I saw and thought and thought
> I listened to the High One's lore.
>
> Of runes I heard it rowned
> rowning them within —
> in the hall of Hár,
> thus I heard them say,
> thus I read them aright.

**Closing:** After the reading is complete, close with the traditional words:

> Now the saws of Hár are said,
> in the hall of Hár!

You will, of course, always want to keep a record of your rune readings, so before returning the lots to their abode, make your records. Then place the staves in their container in silence.

# Taking of Omens

If confirmation of the results of the reading are needed, omens should be taken. This is a traditional part of old Germanic (and Indo-European) divination—the necessity for "corroborating evidence" from another medium. The science of omens (ON *heilar*) is too complex to enter into in any great detail here. The simplest method is to sit in an open area out-of-doors; visualize an enclosed space in front of you (no smaller than ten feet square, but it can be much larger). Then wait for a bird or other animal to enter into, or fly over, that space. For a yes/no confirmation or denial of the validity of any given cast, dark-colored animals or birds (especially black, red, dark blue, or dark brown) mean "yes," and light-colored ones (especially white, light brown, light blue) mean "no."

# 6

# The Ways of Runecasting

THE ALMOST TWO THOUSAND YEAR old description provided by Tacitus gives us a good idea of at least one method of runecasting; however, there are many more based on traditional customs and on cosmological principles which have been used effectively by runecasters. In this chapter we will explore some of the most effective methods, ones that are also most deeply rooted in traditional concepts.

Runecasting, like any precise system of divination—I-Ching, Tarot, astrology—is based on the apparently random superimposition of "meaningful elements" over "meaningful fields." From the combinations and interrelationships of those combinations, the full interpretation is read. In runelore, the runestaves provide the elements of meaning, while the fields of meaning are provided by a number of key cosmological configurations. One of the weaknesses of previous books on runic divination is the general lack of traditional fields of meaning, for in order to know these it is necessary to have in-depth understanding of Germanic cosmology.

Each of the methods presented below may be suited to different kinds of inquiries or explorations as suggested. It is probably best to master one kind of casting first, however, before moving on to wider experimentation. Before setting out to do actual runecastings, you may wish to engage in some reading exercises that will begin to make the runes become more and more "your own."

## Reading Exercise I

Lay out your runelots in the regular futhark order, arranged in the traditional *ætt* pattern as in figure 6.1. Now, begin to make connections between neighboring runes. Go down the first *ætt* F through W, down the second *ætt*, H through S, etc., and try to make a progression out of them. Then reverse this and begin with the third *ætt*, O through T, then with the second *ætt*, S

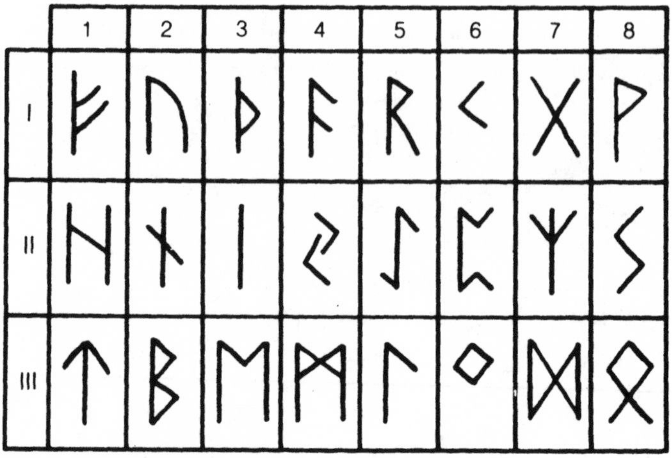

*Figure 6.1. Elder Futhark in ætt arrangement.*

through H, etc., again making meaningful interconnections between and among the runes.

Next, do a similar exercise with the vertical runes across the three *ættir* FHT, UNB, etc., going from top to bottom, and then reversing this from bottom to top. These exercises, which should be done in several different sittings, will strengthen your skills at reading runic contexts. They will also teach you about the living realities of the runic system in a way no book or other person could. This is direct runic learning. You also should begin to realize that the runes find their true meaning in that stead where the outer world runes come face to face with the inner runes of yourself. This process also begins to awaken your inner rune-life. Be sure to write down your results at each sitting.

## Reading Exercise II

The next step in truly "making the runes your own" involves the personal expansion of the meanings of the individual rune-staves. Take one runestave a day and meditate on it. Think deeply about it. Contemplate the relevant rune poem stanzas. Make you own interconnections and come to your own understandings of every rune. As in Exercise I, write down your results. Your finished notes will amount to your own personal and personalized versions of the Runic Tables in chapter 3. These should not be considered set in stone—allow them to grow as you get to know "your runes" better. Remember, these are your personal realizations and may not be valid for others. The Runic Tables were generated in a similar way over a period of some ten years of work informed by the esoteric runic tradition (both ancient and modern).

# On Aspects

One matter crucial to rune reading is determining what aspect of a rune is to be interpreted. Should a lot be read as a bright-stave or as a murk-stave? That the negative aspects of the runes, called *myrkstafir* in Old Norse, were used in magic is beyond question. It also can be safely assumed that such interpretations were responsible for various negative terms presented in chapter 1. Some of the "positive" manifestations of the runes can be said to often have detrimental or dangerous consequences, especially the TH-, H-, N-, I-, and Z-runes. There is no shortage of dark aspects in the rune row. Remember, the runes are your inner advisors, and they must be able to warn you — before it becomes too late to overcome the force of Wyrd.

Aspects are determined in essentially two ways: (1) by the position a runelot falls in a casting (e.g., face up or face down; inside or outside a certain field), and (2) by the angle at which one runelot is juxtaposed to another. This latter method deserves a few introductory remarks. It will be noted that for the most part the runestaves are constructed with acute or obtuse angle combinations, and that there are very few right angles in the shapes. Obtuse angles are known to have a dynamizing effect on the mind, while right angles generally have the opposite effect. (This was a matter of occult study in the late nineteenth and early twentieth century German orders, and is upheld by at least one working Order in America today.) In any event, it is clear that in the runic tradition obtuse or acute angles promote active, positive interaction between and among runes. Right angles create static, negative interaction — or they can block the flow of runic force altogether. They actually cross it.

## DETERMINATION OF ASPECT

In casting, if a rune lands face up it is to be read as a bright-stave; if it lands face down it may either be disregarded in the

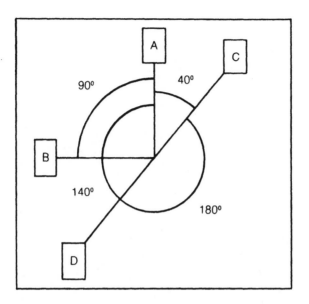

*Figure 6.2. Sample angles for casting aspects.*

reading or read as a murk-stave. The decision on how these lots are to be interpreted must be made before every casting. Also, each runester is encouraged to be consistent in this regard. The usual practice is to disregard them, however. In some casting, runes that fall outside the fields of meaning or off the white cloth also may be read as murk-staves. Again, you must determine how these are to be read beforehand.

When using angular aspects in castings, the runester must measure (at least approximately) the angle at which any two lots in question are juxtaposed. This is done by mentally drawing lines from the two lots through the center point of the cloth, and then determining the angle at which they are juxtaposed. An example of this can be found in figure 6.2. If the result is between 5° and 45°, or between 135° and 360° they are read as bright-staves; if they fall between 45° and 135° they are read as murk-staves. Exact measurements are unnecessary.

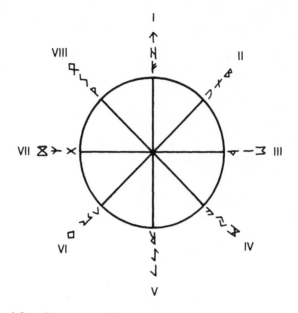

*Figure 6.3. Aett aspectarian.*

Probably the easiest way to see these relationships is by imagining a circle over the cloth that is divided into quarters and bisected by a third line that you will use to orient the rune in question to the the others. Runes falling the the same quarter or in the quarter directly opposite are brightly aspected, while those in the quadrants on either side tend to be murky.

The closer a lot is to the bright angle the more positively it is to be read. Only those close to a 90° relationship should be read as "blockages." Juxtapositions approaching 180° also have a dark aspect, but one which will lead eventually to a positive outcome. In castings these aspects only refine what is already apparent in the reading of the rune and its field. (See Sample Reading 3 on page 104.)

Aspects of this kind are much more useful and easier to determine when using a rune layout method. To determine the relationship among runes in a layout, the runester can refer to figure 6.3, which essentially works on the same principles as the determination of aspects in casting. Let us take the example of *fehu* (F). Runes belonging to the same triad (e.g., F-H-T), or to triads on either side, or to the triads on the same axes as those adjacent to the "home triad" of *fehu* are to be read as bright-staves. Those in the opposite triad are read as murk-staves, but with a positive ultimate outcome. Those runes in triads at a 90° angle, those that cross the axis of the triad in question, are read as murk-staves, usually of a blocking variety. (See Sample Reading 1 on page 94 and Sample Reading 4 on page 108 for clarification of how this works in practice.)

It also should be noted that there is a certain question of "aspect" with regard to the relationship of a given stave to the stead in which it falls or is laid. In the sample readings found below, practical indications of just how this might work are given for various methods. To a great extent intuition must guide the runester in these matters.

The determination of aspect is one of the finer points of the runecaster's skill and craft, and it is one that must be learned through personal experience because the runes will interact differently with different people. Fortunately or unfortunately, it is not a simple matter of reading reversed staves as "bad."

# The Methods

These methods of runecasting are based on "models of meaning" used by the ancient Germanic peoples. It is strongly recommended that you seek to master one of these methods before you begin to work on the others. After a while, you can also begin to experiment with innovative casting or laying techniques. But the traditional modes themselves have something to teach about the "runic mind set." Those who are experienced in other divinatory traditions with "fields of meaning," such as the Tarot or astrology, may wish to experiment with using runes in those contexts. However, they must realize that only part of the runic essence can come through in this manner.

The two classes of operation are casting and laying. The first method discussed here is really a combination of these two types. Castings, because the caster momentarily loses control of the lots, are most effective in reading things in the other world; layings, because the runester is always in control of the lots, are most effective in reading inner states. Both methods have their advantages and disadvantages. In a given casting you may have interest in a certain area of life, yet no lots will fall in that field (which may tell you something as well). On the other hand, with layouts, you will lay lots in steads that may or may not be of equal relevance to your situation – and it takes some skill to intuit which groups of lots are more significant than others.

## 1. THE NORNIC RUNECAST

This method is directly based on the account given by Tacitus in the *Germania* (see chapter 1). The three-fold matrix he mentions is applied to the only obvious three-fold matrix of meaning for Germanic divination: the Urdhr-Verdhandi-Skuld formula.

The runester, following the ritual outline given in chapter 5, randomly casts the lots onto the white cloth, and with his or her eyes closed or diverted upward, blindly picks three lots which he or she lays out in order 1-2-3. To help the runester visualize their relationships, the lots should be laid out in the fashion illustrated in figure 6.4.

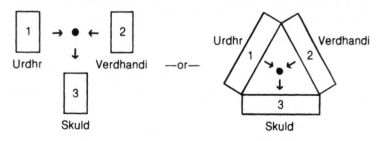

*Figure 6.4. Configuration of lots in the Nornic method.*

Position (1) is the stead of Urdhr (Wyrd), which indicates what is really at the root of the question or problem. It tells what has come about in the past that has conditioned the lot in position (2) – the stead of Verdhandi – which is concerned with the present situation. It tells what is in the process of happening in the present. Both of these are synthesized into the third position – the stead of Skuld – which indicates what should come about in the future given the conditions of the first two positions.

In reading these runes, the vitki may wish to use the aspectarian to determine the quality of their relationships. Inverted or reversed lots may be taken into account, however, this is not necessary.

## READING THE NORNIC RUNECAST

**Object of Inquiry:** Situation surrounding the winning of a new job.

**Reading:** The layout is shown in figure 6.5. *Kenaz* in the Urdhr stead indicates that craft and creativity developed in the past are putting the person in a good position. The groundwork has been laid in a creative fashion. *Dagaz* in Verdhandi shows that the present situation is, however, in a state of flux. Things are

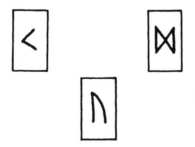

*Figure 6.5. Sample Nornic runecast.*

now dynamic and malleable. The third stave, *uruz* in Skuld, is very hopeful; it indicates that the situation should be formed in accordance with the will of the job seeker. The final stave in this stead also advises "tenacity." The person should persevere with willpower to achieve the right outcome. *Kenaz* is well aspected to *dagaz*, which is in turn well aspected to *uruz*—all of which indicate that the staves are working together smoothly. The *kenaz* is opposed to *uruz*, but because of the otherwise dynamic aspects it seems rather clear that this opposition will be one of a vivifying rather than stultifying kind.

As a matter of fact, the person for whom the reading was done did get the job in question—certainly based on past performance, but also with a little help from magical agencies, and only with the utmost of perseverance.

• • •

The Nornic Runecast may be significantly expanded into the *valknutr* (knot of the slain). This is a sign of the god Ódhinn's ability to bind and unbind fetters of all kinds—including those of "fate." It often is made up of three interlocking triangles (see figure 6.6). To expand the basic nornic reading into the *valknutr*, the runecaster picks three groups of three lots and lays them in interlocking triangles as shown in figure 6.7. The first triangle is an expanded analysis of the Urdhr stead, the second of Verdhandi, and the third of Skuld. This can give a

*Figure 6.6.  The Valknutr.*

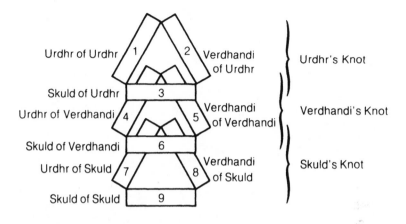

*Figure 6.7. The Valknutr layout.*

more complete picture of what lies at the root of the question, what is happening in the present situation, and what the outcome is likely to be.

## 2. CASTING UPON THE AIRTS METHOD

One of the most well-established arrangements of space into meaningful fields known in the Germanic world is the division of the sky and the plane of the earth into "eighths," in Old Norse *ættir* (which also means generations or families), or in Scots dialect English "airts." In Old Norse these divisions are given the names indicated in figure 6.8. on page 98. Although these names are of Norwegian origin, their inner sense of a four-fold division, expanded by cross-quarter points, fits with a continuing and timeless Germanic pattern. The names indicate that things to the east were more "close in," or earthly, and that things to the west were more "outer," or "far out," and that the main polarity is between north and south. It is no coincidence that the runes also are divided into "eighths."

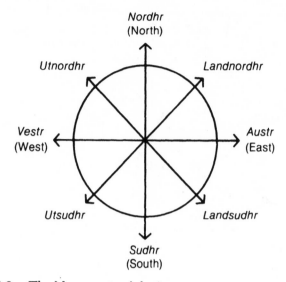

*Figure 6.8. The Norse œttir of the heavens.*

In runecasting this pattern is combined with the other most obvious division of "space," that of the nine worlds of Yggdrasill, to form the design used to divide the casting cloth into fields of meaning illustrated in figure 6.9. (The actual cloth should not have the names of the worlds on it.) In reality, this figure represents the "collapsing" of multidimensional space into a two-dimensional model – as do many sacred symbols of all kinds. The fields are names for the nine worlds of Yggdrasill and derive their meanings from these concepts as shown in Table 6.1 on page 100.

Those lots falling within the inner circles made up of Midhgardhr-Ásgardhr-Hel-Ljóssálfheimr-Svartálfheimr (which in the three-dimensional model make up the vertical column) give a reading of the subjective or psychological state of, or influences on, the person. Those of Ljóssálfheimr and Svartálfheimr are more "personal," while those of Ásgardhr and Hel are more "transpersonal." The lots coming down in the outer fields of Niflheimr-Muspellsheimr-Vanaheimr-Jötunheimr (which together with Midhgardhr form the horizontal plane in

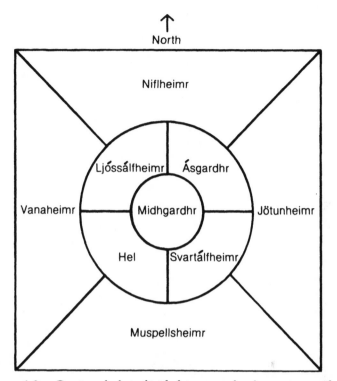

↑
North

Niflheimr

Ljóssálfheimr    Ásgardhr

Vanaheimr    Midhgardhr    Jötunheimr

Hel    Svartálfheimr

Muspellsheimr

*Figure 6.9.   Casting cloth is divided into steads of meaning, and we can see the attribution of the nine worlds to the casting cloth.*

the Yggdrasill model) clarify the state of the objective universe and how it affects the person in question. Note carefully the special synthesizing function of Midhgardhr—the center—where all potentialities are (or can be) manifested.

The runecaster may wish to decorate the cloth with the configuration of lines shown in figure 6.9. Or, you simply may visualize these fields if you are able. Such hidden keys are usually the basis of forms of divination that might seem random at first glance. If the cloth is decorated, it should be embroidered with dark blue or black thread.

Following ritual procedures outlined in chapter 5, the runester blindly casts the lots upon the cloth and then reads them

Table 6.1: Interpretations of the World-Steads

| | |
|---|---|
| Ásgardhr: | Higher influences. Nature of relationship with the divinities. The veiled branches of the question. Matters of honor, positive (active) influences from past states of existence ("incarnations") – *ørlög*. |
| Ljóssálfheimr: | Mental influences. Family matters. Messages of Huginn – directions in which you should plan. What will help you. Paths to help you realize influences from Ásgardhr. |
| Midhgardhr: | The way people come together to manifest themselves in life. The outcome in life. Ego consciousness. |
| Svartálfheimr: | Creative emotional influences. Money matters. Messages from Muninn – things you should reflect on. Paths to realize influences from Hel. |
| Hel: | Hidden or suppressed instinctual desires. Nature of automatic functions or behaviors. The hidden root of the question. Negative (passive, restrictive) influences from past states of existence – *ørlög*. |
| Muspellsheimr: | State of vital energies, that which vitalizes you. Active influences from outside. Things tending toward activity. |
| Niflheimr: | That which resists you. Passive or restrictive influences from the outside. Things tending toward dormancy. |
| Vanaheimr: | Promotes growth. Erotic relationships. Persons of the opposite sex. Balancing influences. Forces of continuity, structure, and well-being. |
| Jötunheimr: | That which confuses you. That which may be left to chance. Things that might test you. Forces pressing for change. Realm of crisis. |

(perhaps sitting on the theal's stool) as they lie on the cloth in their steads of meaning. According to personal custom, lots which land face down may be read as murk-staves or they may be removed from the cloth and set aside. "Inverted" runes cannot be read as such in operations of this kind. Those that fall off the cloth altogether should be disregarded. (Note, however, what these lots are—they may be significant by their absence!)

Once the final configuration has been established, a complex picture may appear. This kind of casting is sometimes so complex that it cannot be fully interpreted at one sitting (especially by beginning runecasters). Therefore, be sure and draw out a record of the casting. You may simply make notes such as ": ᚦ : in Ásgardhr," etc. Often the direction a lot is facing—it may seem to be "pointing to" another lot—gives subtle clues which reveal nuances in the lot's interpretation. For this reason a sketched record is preferred. The true significance of the casting may not be realized until sometime later when you are contemplating the working record.

The pattern resulting from a casting upon the airts can be read in several ways. You may start from what is now manifesting itself in Midhgardhr and work out to the more remotely influential realms, e.g., from Midhgardhr to Ljóssálfheimr and Svartálfheimr, and from this pairing to Ásgardhr and Hel, and from there to the outermost realms of Vanaheimr and Jötunheimr, and Niflheimr and Muspellsheimr. Or, you might reverse this process working from Niflheimr and Muspellsheimr back to Midhgardhr. Ultimately, no linear progression is really inherent in this pattern—it is rather an ultradimensional model. Therefore, intuition may be each runester's best guide.

## SAMPLE CASTING UPON THE AIRTS

**Object of inquiry:** The progress over the coming year of an organization that is dedicated to the discovery and re-discovery of a potent form of magic.

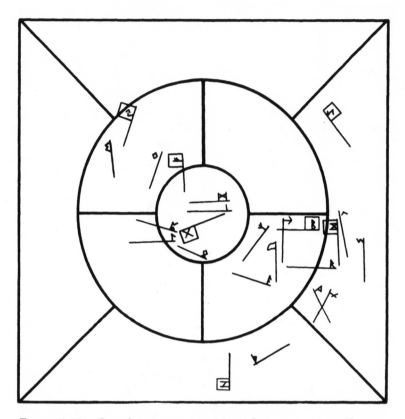

*Figure 6.10. Sample airt casting. Note that square around stave indicates that the lot fell stave side down.*

**Reading:** The layout is shown in figure 6.10. General lack of staves in Vanaheimr indicates no organic tensions are present, while the lack of staves in Niflheimr indicates that there is really no outside pressure or resistance on this group (which is largely secret). The staves in Muspellsheimr, a murky *hagalaz* and a *thurisaz*, both indicate that there are active agents, probably within the consciousness of the various members of the organization, which have been retarding the activization of the organization's programs. These tendencies are, however, very weakly aspected and do not form a strong bundle. Therefore, it would seem that their influence is rather negligible.

A strong bundle is present in Jötunheimr. This indicates that the organization is in dynamic flux, and in many ways is searching for crystallized goals (*sowilo*). The crossing of *nauthiz* and *wunjo* in Jötunheimr suggests that some crisis of an interpersonal nature will lead to positive change. A second crossing between a murky *dagaz* and *kenaz* in Jötunheimr might indicate some confusion in technical matters. However, the favorable juxtaposition of *raidho* counteracts this and leads to a rational, ordered direction into the formative realm of Svartálfheimr. Thus the technical matters will be correctly ordered and put to positive use. The murky *eihwaz* in Jötunheimr is isolated, and therefore seems of little importance. However, it is negatively aspected with the murky *fehu* and *jera* in Ljóssálfheimr, which shows a continuing problem in bringing inspiration to solid fruition.

The bundle in Svartálfheimr would indicate that there will, however, be a great deal of upswelling inspiration which will find formative outlet. The general bundle of so many staves that are indicative of form, shape, and order (*uruz*, *tiwaz*, *raidho*) and divine connection and inspiration (*elhaz* and *ansuz*) in this one field of formative realization would seem to override other indications to the contrary. But, the other indications are reinforced by the presence of the murky B-rune in the midst of this bundle. This clearly indicates that although the formative force and inspiration are powerfully present, they are resisted. This is a warning to be vigilant. Each member of the organization must strive and seek in order for the promise of the A- and Z-runes to bear fruit.

In Ljóssálfheimr there is a loose complex of the E- and NG-runes, which indicates that intellectual development within the organization will be most effective if based on individual inner reflections and/or developed in pairs of persons working on special projects.

Ultimately, it is in the realm of Midhgardhr that the out-come of this magical year is made clear. There are essentially two bundles here. *Mannaz* parallel to *isa* indicates a certain solidifica-tion of the archetypal social organization within the body in question. This is reinforced by the presence of the *othala* in the other bundle, which is closely linked with influences flowing from the dark depths of the hidden realm of Hel (i.e., influences from the past). This influence will be largely unplanned and spontaneous, as indicated by the P-rune, and it will be a truly transformative one, as indicated by the L-rune. Note that both of these lead out of Hel into Midhgardhr and from a bundle with the O-rune and with a murky G-rune. This G-rune, like the B-rune in the bundle found in Svartálfheimr, contains a hidden warning. In this case the warning is to be on the look-out for detrimental influences within the group that could easily arise due to this influx from suprarational realms.

To summarize, it may be said that this organization will be the subject of technical innovation by its members – innovation based on inner reflection and work done between pairs of mem-bers. This innovation will be of a highly inspired nature and it will lead to concrete organizational manifestation. However, all this will not come easily. In every instance there is a "thorn" – some active resistance which will require that all involved be of wakeful wills and hardened hearts.

## 3. LAYING IN THE FUTHARK METHOD

The fixed runic order itself provides us with another traditional way of determining fields of meaning. The runestaves linearly arranged in their three-tiered *ætt* configuration (as presented in figure 6.1) give the steads of interpretation shown in Table 6.2.

The runester may cast the runes onto the cloth, and then take all twenty-four up one by one and lay them in the *ætt* arrangement. Or, you may blindly draw them out of the lot box or bag and then lay them out one through twenty-four in the

Table 6.2: Interpretations of the Stave-Steads

| | | |
|---|---|---|
| 1 | : ᚠ : | Money matters. Psychic energies. |
| 2 | : ᚢ : | Physical health. Vital energies. |
| 3 | : ᚦ : | What opposes you (perhaps physical). |
| 4 | : ᚨ : | Sources of inspiration and intellectual expression. |
| 5 | : ᚱ : | Travels – inner or outer. |
| 6 | : ᚲ : | Creativity. Erotic relationships. |
| 7 | : ᚷ : | What will be given to you. |
| 8 | : ᚹ : | Relationships, friends. What will give you happiness. |
| 9 | : ᚺ : | Area of possible crisis leading to transformation. |
| 10 | : ᚾ : | What resists you (psychically). Source of discontent. |
| 11 | : ᛁ : | What is constraining you. |
| 12 | : ᛃ : | Where rewards can be expected. Relationship with the natural environment. |
| 13 | : ᛇ : | Hidden influences, state of whole being. Relationship with the numinous environment. |
| 14 | : ᛈ : | How you will find joy. |
| 15 | : ᛉ : | Thing that needs attention. Way to the gods. |
| 16 | : ᛋ : | What will guide you. |
| 17 | : ᛏ : | Cognitive state. Legal matters. Ideals. |
| 18 | : ᛒ : | What provides growth and beauty. |
| 19 | : ᛗ : | With what or whom you should work. Erotic relations. |
| 20 | : ᛘ : | Overall psychic state. Attitude toward death. |
| 21 | : ᛚ : | State of emotional balance. What will test you. |
| 22 | : ᛜ : | What you should contemplate. |
| 23 | : ᛞ : | Area of unexpected synchronicity. |
| 24 | : ᛟ : | Greater family matters. National or community issues. |

| 23 | 21 | 19 | 17 | 15 | 13 | 11 | 9 |
|----|----|----|----|----|----|----|----|
| 7  | 5  | 3  | 1  | 2  | 4  | 6  | 8 |
| 10 | 12 | 14 | 16 | 18 | 20 | 22 | 24 |

Figure 6.11.   Layout order of the Futhark method.

*ætt¦* arrangement and in the order shown in figure 6.11. Thus the futhark unfolds from its core and becomes fully manifest in the *ætt¦* configuration. The result will be a complete reading in that all steads will be covered. Aspects may be determined by one of the usual methods outlined on pages 90–93.

Records of these casts are easy to make with notations such as : ᛉ : in : ᚠ :, : ᚲ : in : ᚺ :, : ᛉ : in : ᚦ :, etc. As always, the stead determines the area of life or existence in question, while the lot determines the quality being manifested in that area at the time of the casting or laying. This type of layout is useful for getting a complete reading of your present situation in life. It gives a holistic, synthetic picture, with no real emphasis on outcomes.

### SAMPLE READING OF LAYING IN THE FUTHARK

**Object of inquiry:** General life reading to determine future directions.

**Reading:** The layout is shown in figure 6.12. *Fehu* in the first stead indicates financial affairs are in a state of prosperity. *Othala* in the second stead shows health and vital energies are under control and contained with no positive or negative factors indicated. *Laguz* in the third stead suggests a possible opposition by unconscious forces, while *kenaz* in the fourth stead demon-

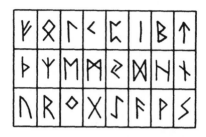

*Figure 6.12. Sample of the Futhark layout method.*

strates a certain inspiration from the creative fire (art). *Perthro* in the fifth stead indicates that travels undertaken will be of an inner kind – along the roads of time and space. The sixth stead occupied by *isa* bodes a shut-down of creativity by icy substance, or an inward turning of creativity to the ego level. *Berkano* in the seventh stead indicates a liberation of energies will occur. *Tiwaz* in the eighth stead points to relationships governed by reason and self-sacrifice (which will ultimately be a source of happiness). *Thurisaz* in the ninth stead points in the direction of a crisis of opposition by hostile reactive forces, while *elhaz* in the tenth stead indicates resistance from archetypal forces within. *Ehwaz* in the eleventh stead betrays an inner constraint. *Mannaz* in the twelfth stead indicates rewards in social stature in essential connections with the gods. (This seems to suggest that the crisis portrayed in the ninth, tenth, and eleventh steads will be overcome.) *Jera* in the thirteenth stead reveals a regular cyclical action in control of hidden influences, while the *dagaz* in the fourteenth stead shows that joy will be found in the experience of subjectivity. *Hagalaz* in the fifteenth stead indicates that attention must be given to the basics, to the seed concepts. (This also seems to relate to the crisis referred to in the ninth, tenth, and eleventh steads.) *Nauthiz* in the sixteenth stead may mean that the subject is being guided by crisis situations (probably through early recognition of the crisis of nine, ten, and eleven). *Uruz* in the seventeenth stead indicates that the cognitive state and ideals are dominated by bullish willpower. *Raidho* in the eighteenth stead shows regularity, rhythm, and motion at work, resulting in growth and beauty. *Ingwaz* in the nineteenth stead suggests that the subject should work alone, gestating within the self. *Gebo* in the twentieth stead indicates a willingness to give and take. *Eihwaz* in the twenty-first stead signifies a "vertical" emotional balance, i.e., emotions dominated by intellect with the likelihood of this tendency increasing. *Ansuz* in the twenty-second stead counsels the subject to meditate on Ódhinn, or the personal divinity within. *Wunjo* in the twenty-third stead points to an unexpected synchronicity in the social field, while *sowilo* in the twenty-fourth stead demonstrates that the subject's current goals are in the social field itself.

The overall counsel of this reading to the subject is that in matters of basic security all is well. The principal opposition is within. This can be overcome by establishing firmer, more regular links with the personal divinity. If the subject develops inner connections he will be rewarded with outer successes.

## 4. THE SEVEN REALMS LAYING

The ancient Norse often talked of seven realms of sentient beings from which information could be gained—if one but knew the "language" of that realm. This tradition is only imperfectly transmitted in the "Alvísmál" of the *Poetic Edda*, where seven realms are mentioned but only six are ever used in any one stanza. These stanzas were composed to reveal the secret poetic languages used in the realms of the AEsir, Vanir, elves, dwarves, etins, as well as among the dead, and among people in Midhgardhr. As Hollander notes in his introduction to the "Alvísmál," the poem represents a late and confused state of affairs. But it reflects an ancient cosmological order which only needs a slight adjustment provided by the Yggdrasill key to make it intelligible. Only seven of the nine worlds of Yggdrasill spawn sentient beings—Muspellsheimr and Niflheimr are devoid of consciousness as raw forces of "nature." The runes are

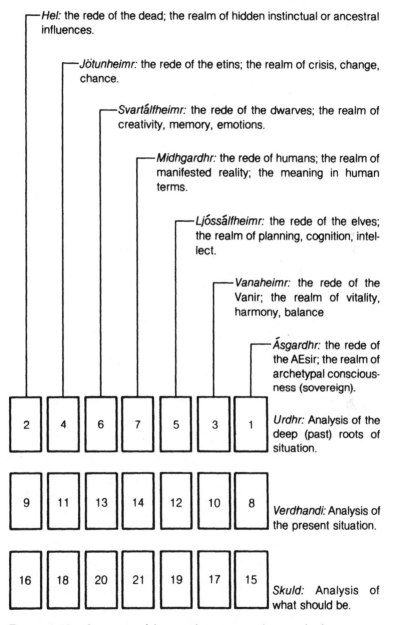

*Hel:* the rede of the dead; the realm of hidden instinctual or ancestral influences.

*Jötunheimr:* the rede of the etins; the realm of crisis, change, chance.

*Svartálfheimr:* the rede of the dwarves; the realm of creativity, memory, emotions.

*Midhgardhr:* the rede of humans; the realm of manifested reality; the meaning in human terms.

*Ljóssálfheimr:* the rede of the elves; the realm of planning, cognition, intellect.

*Vanaheimr:* the rede of the Vanir; the realm of vitality, harmony, balance

*Ásgardhr:* the rede of the AEsir; the realm of archetypal consciousness (sovereign).

*Urdhr:* Analysis of the deep (past) roots of situation.

*Verdhandi:* Analysis of the present situation.

*Skuld:* Analysis of what should be.

*Figure 6.13. Layout and key to the seven realms method.*

one mode of communication between and among these sentient realms.

Note that the principle behind the layout pattern is that which underlies the cosmogonic process in Germanic lore: the continuing synthesis of polar opposites leading to transformation. This is superimposed upon the nornic process to give a picture of the layers of action or forces at work through time.

Following your ritual procedure, draw twenty-one runes from the box or bag and lay them out in the order indicated in figure 6.13. These lots are then to be interpreted according to the key shown in figure 6.13. This layout pattern is most useful for complete self-analyses, and in many ways represents a more "controlled" version of the method of casting upon the airts.

This kind of reading will be improved as you become more knowledgeable about the realms. Also refer to the discussion of these realms under the Casting Upon the Airts Method as well as in chapter 6 of *Runelore*. Each lot stead is read quite simply as a bringing together of the nornic process with the realms of sentient beings. At each level the row is synthesized in the Midhgardhr stead, so that lot steads seven, fourteen, and twenty-one are the ultimate keys to the reading. The three lots excluded from the reading also may be significant by their absence.

## SAMPLE READING IN THE SEVEN REALMS METHOD

**Object of Inquiry:** Analysis of the ultimate effect of disruptive personality within an esoteric organization.

**Reading:** The layout is shown in figure 6.14. *Ehwaz* and *fehu* in the outer levels (Ásgardhr and Hel) of Urdhr indicate that sexual energy and erotic relationships are at the ultimate root of the question. There is a general freezing of vital forces shown by *isa* in Vanaheimr. An intense level of emotional crisis and conflict is evidenced by *nauthiz* in Jötunheimr. This is, perhaps, the

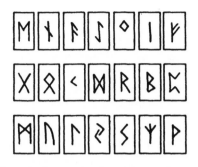

*Figure 6.14. Sample layout in the seven realms method.*

result of a general lack of vitality coupled with an uncontrolled influx of sexual energies. The ability of all parties to think clearly is in a state of stasis (or perhaps gestation) indicated by the *ingwaz* in Ljóssálfheimr. This also could mean that certain plans are waiting to be hatched. However, the AEsiric powers also seem to have had a hand in shaping things, as intimated by *ansuz* in Svartálfheimr. The basis of the present situation is rather ambivalent; there seems to be a "velocity toward manifestation."

The present unsettled elements are in archetypal flux, as shown by the presence of *perthro* in the Ásgardhr of Verdhandi. This can bode well if higher counsel is heeded in a state of spiritual detachment – do not act further. In the root of things, as shown by the *gebo* in Hel, honor and credit of those in this state will be preserved. Vitality is strongly disciplined and held in protected reserve, indicated by *berkano* in Vanaheimr. The social aspect of *othala* is in great confusion due to its position in Jötunheimr. The present state of crisis shown by othala's presence in Jötunheimr is rooted in *nauthiz* in the Urdhr level. Fortunately, rational control (*raidho*) is reinforced in the intellectual realm of Ljóssálfheimr. The presence of *kenaz* in Svartálfheimr may also indicate that craft is being wielded in the creative realm. *Dagaz* in the Midhgardhr of Verdhandi remains ambiguous, as its light may be dimmed by the poor aspect of *raidho* to *dagaz*.

The pairing of *manna* and *wunjo* in the archetypal realms of Skuld seems ideal. This appears to indicate that ultimately there will be an outcome based upon divine principles in a joyous atmosphere. *Elhaz* in Vanaheimr shows a certain upward sweep of vitality, while *uruz* in Jötunheimr suggests that the chaos will be reformed. Cognitive plans will reach their right goals, demonstrated by the presence of *sowilo* in Ljóssálfheimr, and there will be creativity according to law. *Uruz* and *laguz* in Jötunheimr and Svartálfheimr respectively seem to indicate a certain reformation of order out of the chaos and crisis that was rooted in *nauthiz* in the Jötunheimr of Urdhr.

The final outcome is exemplary. *Jera* indicates that right rewards will be gained for beneficial past actions (or non-action). The aspect of the whole of the Skuld realm could not be more hopeful. Ultimately, this disruptive influence will have nothing but a strengthening effect on the social circle – but there may be more rough seas ahead as Verdhandi transits to Skuld.

## Alternate Ways of Drawing Lots

In all the methods outlined above the runester is limited to reading each rune only once in every laying of the lots. However, this may not produce the most accurate reading since it is quite possible that a rune could be manifest in more than one stead.

Following are two more ways of generating lots. When using the first method you draw a lot from your bag or box and, depending on which layout pattern you are working with, trace that rune on paper or in the ground in a specially prepared section of loose earth. Put the lot back in the bag or box again and shake it, saying aloud or silently, "Urdhr-Verdhandi-Skuld." Then draw another lot from the box and note it in its proper stead. Continue until you have completed the pattern. Theoretically, you could end up with a reading that contains only one rune!

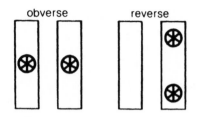

*Figure 6.15. The ætt staves.*

The second method involves the use of an archaic form of Germanic "dice." In order to use this technique, the runester must construct eight staves that are broad and flat enough that they can only land with one face up when cast upon a flat surface. Two of these staves, the *ætt*-staves, will be marked (for example with a six-spoked wheel) on one side, one will be blank on the reverse, and the other will be marked with two signs on the reverse as shown in figure 6.15. Casting these staves naturally will result in a number 1, 2, or 3. These will give the /*ætt*-count of a particular rune.

A second set of six staves, the lot staves, is to be prepared with another kind of marking (for example a dot or circle). Four of these have only one mark on one side; one of them has two marks on one side. The reverse of the other five staves are blank. The sixth stave has two marks on one side and one on the reverse. (See figure 6.16.)

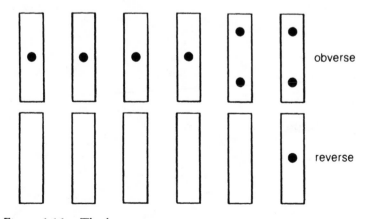

*Figure 6.16. The lot staves.*

Any casting of these lots will result in a number between one and eight. These determine the particular lot or rune within the already determined *ætt*. This system works on the same binary code as the "secret runes."[1]

First you cast the *ætt*-staves and get a number from one to three, then the lot staves, to get a number between one and eight. The resulting combination, e.g., 3:6 identifies as particular runestave in the Futhark order—in this case *laguz*, the sixth rune in the third *ætt*.

As each runestave is generated in this manner, note it in its proper stead so you can interpret it according to the kind of reading being done. The same runestave can occur several times in the same reading. Runes that would have been "constrained" to appear in the full "Futhark Layout" may be significantly absent in this type of reading. These methods allow for the element of free play that usually is absent in layout methods.

## Yes/No Answers

Probably the most instinctive use of divinatory technique is that of trying to get a "yes" or a "no" answer to a question, e.g., the "he loves me he loves me not" game with the petals of a flower. The runestaves can provide such answers—and something more besides.

In the customary ritual framework, cast the runes upon the cloth with the airt/Yggdrasill pattern. The only significant pattern for this reading is the outer circle (enclosing the vertical fields of Ásgardhr-Hel-Svartálfheimr-Ljóssálfheimr-Midh gardhr). Disregard the lots that fall outside the outer circle. Only those totally within the "circle of advisors" are to be read. If the majority of these are face up, the answer is "yes"; if the majority are face down, the answer is "no." The ratio of "yes"-

---

[1]Edred Thorsson, *Runelore: A Handbook of Esoteric Runology* (York Beach, ME: Samuel Weiser, 1987): 87–91.

staves to "no"-staves gives you some idea of how "close the call is." An equal number of yeses and nos is, of course, no decision. (But this is the reading—do not try to ask the same question again until the next day.)

This kind of reading also gives you some indications of the "why" of the answer. Reversed lots may tell you the aspects that need to be reversed, if possible, to get an affirmative outcome.

The ritual element in this kind of reading is very important. Because it is a "hit or miss" kind of operation, the runester must evoke a strong sense of being "in sync" with the runes before such a casting can be used seriously.

# List of Abbreviations

All translations from Old Norse, Old English, and other older languages found in this book are those of the author. An attempt has been made to strike a balance between poetic and literal translation, but often favor is given to the literal for the sake of correct understanding. In such cases notes may be added. All references to stanzas in the *Poetic Edda* are keyed to the translation by Lee M. Hollander, however, translations are taken directly from the original text as edited by Gustav Neckel and Hans Kuhn.

| | |
|---|---|
| B.C.E. | Before the Common Era (=/ B.C.) |
| C.E. | Common Era (=/A.D.) |
| Gmc. | Germanic |
| Go. | Gothic |
| MS(S) | manuscript(s) |
| OE | Old English |
| OHG | Old High German |
| ON | Old Norse |
| pl. | plural |
| sg. | singular |

# Transliteration of Old Norse and Germanic Terms

Certain special Germanic graphics have been transliterated in this book. The following are in keeping with certain spelling conventions of the Middle Ages.

| | |
|---|---|
| ð | dh |
| þ | th |
| ǫ | ö |

# Pronunciation of Old Norse

The phonetic values provided below are those of reconstructed Old Norse (as it would have been spoken in the Viking Age).

The consonants b, d, f, l, m, t, and v are the same in modern English.

| | |
|---|---|
| a | s in "artistic" |
| á | as in "father" |
| e | as in "men" |
| é | as ay in "bay" |
| i | as in "it" |
| í | as ee in "feet" |
| o | as in "omit" |
| ó | as in "ore" |
| ö | as in "not" |
| ø | pronounced same as ö |
| u | as in "put" |
| ú | as in "rule" |
| ae | as ai in "hair" |
| oe | as u in "slur" |
| y | as u in German Hütee (i with rounded lips) |
| ý | as u in German Tür (ee with rounded lips) |
| au | as ou in "house" |
| ei | as ay in "May," or as i in "mine" |
| ey | pronounced same as ei |
| g | always hard as in "go" |
| ng | as in "long" |
| h | same as English, except before consonants, then as wh in "where" |
| j | always as y in "year" |
| p | as in English, except before t; then this pt cluster is pronounced ft |
| r | trilled r |
| s | always voiceless as in "sing" |

th      voiceless th as in "thin"
dh      voiced th as in "the"
rl       pronounced dl
rn      pronounced dn
nn     pronounced dn after long vowels and diphthongs

# Glossary

AEsir: sg. Áss, genitive pl. Ása (used as a prefix to denote that the god or goddess is "of the AEsir") ON. Race of gods corresponding to the functions of magic, law, and war.

ætt: pl. ættir ON. Family or genus, used both as a name for the threefold divisions of the futhark and the eight divisions of the heavens. Also means a group or division of eight.

airt: Scots dialect word. See ætt.

Aptrburdhr: ON. Rebirth. This is the ancient Germanic idea similar to reincarnation. It is the rebirth of the essential characterisitics of the ancestors along genetic lines.

athling: OE. A noble person motivated by noble goals and tasks.

bright-stave: From ON heidh-rún. The positive aspects of a given runestave.

Edda: ON. Word of uncertain origin, used as the title of ancient manuscripts dealing with mythology. The Elder or Poetic Edda is a collection of poems composed betwee 800 and 1270 C.E., while the Younger or Prose Edda was written by Snorri Sturluson in 1222 C.E. as a codification of the mythology of Ásatrú for the skalds.

Erulian: Member of the ancient gild of runemasters who formed an inter-tribal network of initiates in the Germanic mysteries.

etin: Developed from OE eoten and ON jötunn. A type of "giant" known for its stength. Also a generic name for "giant" (in ON Jötunheimr, etc.).

etin-wife: A female etin taken in magical marriage.

formáli: pl. formálar. ON. Formulaic speeches used to load action with magical intent.

fylgja: pl. fylgjur ON. A numinous being attached to every individual, which is the repository of all past action and which accordingly affects the person's life; the personal divinity. Visualized as a contrasexual entity, an animal, or an abstract shape.

galdr: pl. galdrar. ON Originally "incantation," the verb *gala* is used also for "to crow"; later meant magic in general, but especially verbal magic.

Germanic: (1) The proto-language spoken by the Germanic peoples before the various dialects (e.g., English, German, Gothic, Scandinavian) developed; also a collective term for the languages belonging to this group. (2) A collective term for all peoples descended from the Germanic-speaking group (e.g., the English, the Germans, the Scandinavians). Norse or Nordic is a subgroup of Germanic and refers only to the Scandinavian branch of the Germanic heritage.

godhi: ON. A priest in the ancient religion of Ásatrú.

gydhja: ON. Feminine form of *godhi*.

harrow: Traditional Germanic word for an altar (ON form: *horg*). Originally this referred to an outdoor altar made of stone.

hugauga: ON. The mind's eye used for purposes of magical visualization. Identical with the *ājña chakra*, or "third eye."

murk-stave: From ON *myrkstafr*. The negative aspects of a given runestave.

Norn: pl. Nornir (or English Norns) ON. One of the three complex cosmic beings in female form that embody the mechanical process of cause and effect and serve as a matrix for evolutionary force.

Odian: A technical term for the "theology" of the Erulian. Distinguished from the Odinist by the fact that the Odian does not worship Ódhinn but seeks to emulate his pattern of self-transformation.

Old English: The language spoken by the Anglo-Saxon tribes in southern Britain from about 450-1100 C.E. Also known as Anglo-Saxon.

Old Norse: The language spoken by West Scandinavians (in Norway, Iceland, and parts of Britian) in the Viking Age (ca. 800-1100). Also the language of the *Eddas* and of skaldic poetry. After about 1100 we can speak of Old Norwegian as the language of Norway and Old Icelandic as that of Iceland proper.

ørlög: ON. The Germanic concept of "fate," which is based on the idea that the present (and hence any contingent "future") is conditioned by actions "laid down" in the past. The word literally means "primal layers."

runecasting: An operation of runic divination, especially one in which the runelots are thrown onto the casting cloth.

runecraft: The use of rune skill (esoteric knowledge) for causing changes in the objective environment.

rune laying: An operation of runic divination in which the lots are not thrown, but rather laid in their steads of meaning.

runelot: Same as runestave, except used exclusively here to mean a runestave used in divinatory operations.

rune skill: Intellectual knowledge of runelore.

runestave: The physical shape of a runic character, or the physical object onto which the shape is carved (especially when fashioned from wood).

runester: From ON *rýnstr*, "one most skilled in runes." General term for one involved in deep-level rune skill.

runework: The use of rune skill for causing changes or development in the subjective universe; self-developmental work.

stead (of meaning): The field on the casting cloth or imaginary slot in which a lot is cast or laid and which provides the context of meaning and interpretation for the lot.

taufr: ON. Talismanic magic. Also used to refer to the talismanic object itself.

theal's stool: The stool or chair upon which the runecaster sits when interpreting runelots. "Theal" is a modern English version of the OE *thyle*, and ON *thulr*.

thurs: pl thursar. From ON *thurs*. A "giant" characterized by great strength and age, e.g., the rime-thurses or "frost-giants."

valkyrja: pl. valkýrjur ON. "Chooser of the Fallen" (i.e., the slain). Protective *fylgja*-like numinous qualities that become attached to certain persons who attract them; a linking force between humans and gods (especially Ódhinn).

Vanir: sg. Van ON. The race of gods corresponding to the fertility, prosperity, eroticism functions.

World: (1) The entire cosmos or universe. (2) One of the nine levels of being or planes of existence that make up the ordered cosmos.

wyrd: Modern English "weird." (ON form: *urdhr*, also the name of the first Great Norn). The process in which past actions (*ǿrlög*) work through time to affect present experience.

Yggdrasill: ON. The cosmic tree of nine worlds or planes of the multiverse.

# Bibliography

Bates, Brian. *The Way of Wyrd*. San Francisco: Harper and Row, 1983.

Blum, Ralph. *The Book of Runes*. New York: St. Martin's Press, 1982.

Caesar, Julius. *The Conquest of Gaul*. Harmondsworth, UK: Penguin, 1951.

Davidson, H. R. Ellis. "The Germanic World." In: Michael Loewe and Carmen Blacker, eds. *Oracles and Divination*. Boston, MA: Shambhala, 1981.

Flowers, Stephen E. *Runes and Magic: Magical Formulaic Elements in the Older Runic Tradition*. Berne: Lang, 1986.

Franz, Marie-Louise von. *On Divination and Synchronicity: The Psychology of Meaningful Chance*. Toronto: Inner City Books, 1980.

Hollander, Lee M. *The Poetic Edda*. Austin, TX: University of Texas Press, 1962, 2nd ed.

Howard, Michael. *The Runes and Other Magical Alphabets*. York Beach, ME: Samuel Weiser, 1978.

———. *The Magic of the Runes*. Wellingborough, UK: Aquarian Press, 1980.

Jossé, Roland Dionys. *Die Tala der Raunen (Runo-astrologische Kabbalistik) Handbuch der Deutung des Wesens und Weges eines Menschen auf Grund der in seinem Namen verborgenen Sckicksalsraunen*. Freiburg: Bauer, 1955.

Jung, Carl G. *Synchronicity: An Acausal Connecting Principle*. Princeton: Princeton University Press, 1973.

Kosbab, Werner. *Das Runen-Orakel*. Freiburg: Bauer, 1982.

Kurtzahn, E. Tristan. *Die Runen als Heilszeichen und Schicksalslose*. Bad Oldesloe: Uranus, 1924.

Line, David and Julia. *Fortune-Telling by Runes*. Wellingborough, UK: Aquarian Press, 1984.

Mercer, Beryl and Tricia Bramwell. *The Anglo-Saxon Runes*. Amber, UK: Phoenix Runes, 1983.

Much, Rudolf. *Die Germania des Tacitus*. Heidelberg: Carl Winter, 1967, 2nd ed.

Neckel, Gustav and Hans Kuhn. *Edda. Die Lieder des Codex Regius nebst verwandten Denkmälern*. Heidelberg: Carl Winter, 1962, 3rd ed.

Osborn, Marijane and Stella Longland. *Rune Games*. London: Routledge and Kegan Paul, 1982.

Pushong, Carlyle A. *Rune Magic*. London: Regency, 1978.

Spiesberger, Karl. *Runenmagie*. Berlin: Schikowski, 1955.

Tacitus, Cornelius. *The Agricola and the Germania*. Harmondsworth, UK: Penguin, 1948.

Thorsson, Edred. *Futhark: A Handbook of Rune Magic*. York Beach, ME: Samuel Weiser, 1984.

———. *Runelore: A Handbook of Esoteric Runology*. York Beach, ME: Samuel Weiser, 1987.

Willis, Tony. *Runic Workbook*. Wellingborough, UK: Aquarian Press, 1986.

# Index

# About the Author

Edred Thorsson received his doctorate in Germanic Languages and Medieval Studies from the University of Texas. He translated Guido von List's *The Secret of Runes*, taught humanities at the university level, and founded Runa-Raven Press. He is the author of *Futhark: A Handbook of Rune Magic* and *Runelore*. He lives near Austin, Texas. Visit him online at *www.runaraven.com*.